Privacy, Intimacy, and Isolation

PRIVACY, INTIMACY, AND ISOLATION

Julie C. Inness

New York   *Oxford*
OXFORD UNIVERSITY PRESS
1992

Oxford University Press

Oxford   New York   Toronto
Delhi   Bombay   Calcutta   Madras   Karachi
Kuala Lumpur   Singapore   Hong Kong   Tokyo
Nairobi   Dar es Salaam   Cape Town
Melbourne   Auckland

and associated companies in
Berlin   Ibadan

Published by Oxford University Press, Inc.
200 Madison Avenue, New York, NY 10016

Oxford is a registered trademark of Oxford University Press

Library of Congress Cataloging-in-Publication Data
Inness, Julie C.
Privacy, intimacy, and isolation / Julie Inness.
p. cm.   Includes bibliographical references and index.
ISBN 0-19-507148-4
1. Privacy   2. Intimacy (Psychology)   3. Privacy,
Right of—United States.   I. Title.
BF575.P93I56 1992   155.9'2—dc20   91-28191

1 3 5 7 9 8 6 4 2

Printed in the United States of America
on acid-free paper

For my parents

PREFACE

Robert Bork's ultimately unsuccessful Supreme Court confirmation hearings presented me with a dilemma about privacy. Those opposed to his nomination argued that Bork would undermine legal protection for one of our most cherished interests: privacy. By doing so, Bork would leave a wide range of privacy claims without legal support, claims covering such diverse issues as abortion, contraceptives, and access to the home. In response to this criticism, I initially expected Bork's supporters to deny that he would endanger the constitutionally protected right to privacy. Curiously enough, many of them failed to do this; in fact, they argued that Bork ought to attack the notion, stripping it of constitutional sanction. To support this contention, they pointed out that a right to privacy is not stated in the Constitution; furthermore, they argued that privacy is neither conceptually nor morally separable from other legally protected interests, such as liberty from undue state intervention. The conflicting stances of Bork's supporters and opponents constituted the core of my dilemma. On the one hand, I wished to retain privacy, since it seemed to protect so many vital areas of life. On the other hand, I realized that I was unclear about what I meant by "privacy." I could neither define it nor explain its value. My book emerged in response to this dilemma. It embodies my concern that our vital privacy claims might diminish under skeptical attacks, perhaps even vanish, unless supported by a strong theoretical foundation.

Faced with this threat, I originally turned to the legal and philosophical literature on privacy, seeking to understand its conceptual and normative underpinnings. However, I discovered that both are marked by an unusual amount of heated disagreement, a fact publicized during Bork's confirmation hearings. These disagreements cover considerable ground, ranging from privacy's conceptual independence from other interests to its definition and the source of its value. To resolve such numerous, crucial conflicts, I decided to explore privacy for myself. It seemed to me that the following three questions needed answers before privacy could possess a sound theoretical foundation: Is privacy conceptually and morally separable from other interests? How should it be defined? What value should it be accorded? These questions are at the core of this work.

The Bork hearings did not totally undermine my privacy intuitions; I was left with the sense that our interest in privacy cannot be collapsed into other interests. I was also left with the feeling that any satisfactory definition of the term would have to be capable of linking together the apparently divergent issues collected together under the rubric ''privacy,'' issues involving information, access, and intimate decisions. Finally, I still believed that privacy was correctly accorded a positive normative value. The conclusions I reach in this work support these initial intuitions. After disposing of skepticism about privacy, I argue that privacy provides the agent with control over intimate decisions, including decisions about intimate access, the dissemination of intimate information, and intimate actions. I understand intimacy to be a product of the agent's motivation. To claim that something is intimate is to claim that it draws its meaning and value for the agent from the emotions of love, liking, or care. Hence, I conclude that privacy is the state of possessing control over decisions concerning matters that draw their meaning and value from an agent's love, liking, or care. We value the control privacy provides because it embodies our respect for persons as emotional choosers. To respect others in this fashion, we must acknowledge their autonomous capacity for love, liking, and care: we must accord them privacy. Understanding the ties between privacy and intimacy allows us to understand the paramount importance of protecting privacy: a person without privacy is a person who cannot live by her own plans with respect to intimacy, a person who has been denied control over her emotional destiny.

While ideas may flourish in privacy, they do not develop in isolation; my thoughts about privacy are no exception. I wish to extend my sincere thanks to my colleagues, without whom I could not have undertaken this project. I am grateful for the support provided by my fellow philosophers at Stanford University, where I started this work, especially those members of the Philosophy Department who commented on it. The Humanities Center at Stanford provided me with congenial, interdisciplinary support; I cannot imagine a better place to spend a year writing. My deep gratitude is also extended to the members of the Department of Philosophy at Mount Holyoke College, especially Tom Wartenberg. Teaching has always stimulated my thoughts, so I must thank all my fine students at Mount Holyoke for continually reminding me of the pleasures of philosophy. Finally, an earlier version of Chapter 5 was published as "Information, Access, or Intimate Decisions About One's Actions? The Content of Privacy" in *Public Affairs Quarterly* 5 (1991): 227–242; my thanks goes to the editor for allowing me to use this work.

My especial thanks, along with my deepest appreciation, belongs to those who have been there for me every step of the way. Without my friends, I would have taken myself far too seriously to ever have placed a word on paper. Many of my students have also been supportive, many more than I could list; you are the best possible students and friends. A special thanks goes to Beth for persistently nudging me closer to my computer and the possibility of writing. Finally, without my family, I would have never been in the position to commence this work in the first place. Their support will always be invaluable.

South Hadley, Mass. J. C. I.
August 1991

CONTENTS

Privacy, Intimacy, and Isolation

1

Introduction:
The Chaotic World of Privacy

Exploring the concept of privacy resembles exploring an unknown swamp. We start on firm ground, noting the common usage of "privacy" in everyday conversation and legal argument; it seems it will be a simple task to locate the conceptual and moral core of such an often-used term. But then the ground softens as we discover the confusion underlying our privacy intuitions. We find intense disagreement about both trivial and crucial issues; for example, one person contends that the state would violate her privacy if it compelled her to wear a seat belt, yet the state argues that privacy has nothing to do with the wearing of seat belts,[1] and another argues that the state would violate his privacy if it interfered with his homosexual sexual activities, while the government contends that privacy's scope covers only heterosexual sexual activities.[2] At this point, we turn to the legal and philosophical literature on privacy in the hope of gaining a foothold. Instead, we find chaos; the literature lacks an accepted account of privacy's definition and value. Given our muddled state, we might initially try to escape by withdrawing—do we truly need an unified account of privacy? Although retreat may be appealing, I believe we cannot abandon the concept of privacy to confusion without significant loss. If we wish to avoid extending this elusive notion to cover too much of our lives or, perhaps worse, shrinking it to cover too little, we must come to understand it. Because of this conviction, I seek to construct an escape route from the quagmire: a definition of privacy and an explanation of its value that will clarify and resolve our conflicts.

Before discussing how an acceptable account of privacy might be constructed, we must answer a preliminary question: why is the concept

3

important enough to merit theoretical concern in the first place? I could respond with an appeal to the value of conceptual tidiness, but this response does not adequately explain its importance. Privacy demands attention because it is both an immensely powerful and hotly contested interest. The power of privacy is seen in the variety of issues that legal courts have placed under its protection, issues that range from who should have access to an agent's home or bank account number to decisions about contraceptives, sexuality, and abortion.[3] Despite the pervasive legal reach of privacy, privacy claims are often challenged in the realm of the law and everyday life.[4] Disagreements about privacy cover considerable ground. On the one hand, many people accept the existence of privacy, but disagree about the matters belonging within its purview; for example, some contend that abortion should be protected by the constitutional right to privacy, while others reject this contention. Similarly, some suggest that privacy protects consenting sexual activity, while others deny this. On the other hand, the existence of privacy itself is contested; although many accept its importance, there are those who wish to see claims to privacy banished entirely on the grounds that an independent moral interest in privacy does not exist.

Of course, the fact we disagree about many important privacy-related issues does not mean privacy needs philosophical attention. Its widely contested nature might be attributed to either ideological differences about unrelated matters or disagreements about facts. Accordingly, we would expect liberals and libertarians to argue about privacy claims due to their conflicting views of state power. Similarly, the state's refusal to extend the protection of privacy over homosexual activity might be due to its prejudiced views concerning the supposedly harmful nature of such conduct. However, such disagreements cannot be explained away by appealing to extraneous considerations. Although certain debates on privacy may be resolvable without directly addressing questions about the concept, the majority of these conflicts are intimately related to the disorder of the implied privacy theories underlying the conflicting positions. Claims about privacy and their counterclaims are often based on conflicting definitions of privacy and accounts of its function and its value. Some people believe that decisions about abortion fall within the scope of privacy since they assume that privacy protects intimate decisions; others deny this, arguing that privacy only regulates the dissemination of information. Some see privacy as often equivalent to unwanted isolation because they do not view it as intrinsically desirable; others disagree, assuming that privacy possesses a normatively positive value, one incompatible with the normatively negative state of undesired isolation. If we are to resolve the wide range of applied privacy issues, we must start by disentangling the conflicting theories that support the opposing positions, then move on to privacy's correct definition and the true nature of its function and value.

Four questions need to be answered if we are to develop a satisfactory theory of privacy: first, can we extract an adequate account of privacy from the legal and philosophical literature? A critical literature survey might limit our privacy disagreements; however, our confusion might prove intractable if no clearly acceptable account of privacy emerged. We would then have to develop a new definition, extracting its components from everyday experience, privacy law, and privacy theory. In examining this melange, we must try to understand the mechanism by which privacy works. Thus, our second question concerns the nature of the relation privacy establishes between the agent and the external world: what is the function of privacy? But, since privacy clearly establishes a relation between *part* of the agent's life and the world at large, we must address a third question about the realm being protected: what is the content of privacy? An account of how privacy functions combined with an explanation of its content will produce a complete definition of privacy. This definition will enable us to see the common conceptual threads of our everyday and legal privacy claims, but it will not provide us with an explanation of the moral significance of those claims, which leads us to the fourth question: what is the nature and source of the value we accord to privacy? Although it is clear how to set about answering the first question, this is not self-evident for the others. Some additional explanation is required.

When I experience privacy with respect to something such as my room or diary, I stand in a particular relation to my room or diary, a relation I do not stand in with respect to the entire external world. More formally, I have privacy with respect to X if and only if I stand in relation R to X. However, the nature of this relation, which I will term the "function of privacy," is not clear. Two plausible accounts capture our intuitions, yet they have radically different implications as far as the nature of privacy is concerned. On the one hand, privacy might be antithetical to publicity: it might function by separating the individual from others, restricting the access others have to particular areas of her life.[5] Accordingly, a claim to privacy becomes a claim to have these areas of life separated from the world. When I make a privacy assertion about my diary or room, I am asserting that they are not to be accessed by others. Even an individual trapped in the unwanted isolation of an uninhabited island experiences privacy—her life is not accessed by others. On the other hand, privacy might not necessarily be opposed to publicity: its function might be to provide the individual with control over certain aspects of her life. Accordingly, a claim to privacy becomes a claim to control these areas of life. I experience privacy with respect to my diary or room when I am capable of controlling access to them. An individual experiences privacy on an uninhabited island if she is capable of controlling access to it. As these examples reveal, separation and control-based accounts delineate sharply different realms of privacy; the conditions under which privacy is, or is not, experienced will affect what counts as a justified claim. Given these differing implications, clearly an initial step toward a definition of privacy is to determine whether privacy separates areas of the agent's life from the public sphere or provides her with control over them. The next step is to explore the content of these privacy-protected areas.

Abortion decisions, computer accounts, sex, love letters, contraceptive decisions, the body, the home, bank balances—this is only the start of a list of the heterogenous matters claimed under the rubric, "privacy." Despite its diversity, this collection reveals the nature of the three central debates about the content of privacy. The first may be termed the information/access versus decisional privacy debate. On the one hand, privacy is claimed to involve the agent regulating information about or access to herself, access to love letters, computer accounts, and the body all being quintessential privacy matters. On the other hand, privacy is claimed to involve the agent's freedom to make certain decisions about her own actions in matters involving contraceptives, sexuality, abortion, and child rearing. The second debate concerns the nature of the information, access, or decisions about actions contained within the scope of privacy. Privacy might protect *all* information about an agent, access to the agent, or decisions about her own actions; by this account, privacy protects grocery lists as well as love letters and decisions about wearing a seat belt as well as those about abortion. But we need not accept this broad scope; privacy might involve only *intimate* information, access, or decisions, such as the contents of love letters, personal areas of the body, and decisions about sexuality. If so, we are faced with a third debate, which focuses on different attempts to characterize intimacy, either in terms of behavior or in terms of its underlying motivations; for example, is sexual behavior intimate simply *qua* sexual behavior, or does its intimacy lie in the love it often conveys? These three debates must be resolved because their resolution fundamentally changes not only the scope of justified privacy claims, but also our account of privacy's value; for example, we will likely accord a different value to protecting a realm of intimate decisions than to protecting a realm of nonintimate decisions. With this, we can take our final step toward a satisfactory account of privacy: developing an explanation of its normative force.

Privacy is usually considered a moral interest of paramount importance. Its loss provokes talk of violation, harm, and loss of agency. Paradoxically privacy is also described as a condition from which we should flee, promoting isolation, deprivation, and separation. It possesses the potential to entrap the powerless, eliminating their recourse to the public sphere. To illustrate, consider how battered women might suffer from respecting the privacy of the home, which might be incompatible with acknowledging the needs of these women. This tension between those who praise privacy and those who condemn it leads to our fourth and final question: what is the nature and source of the value we accord to privacy as a moral interest or right? Before we can answer, we must respond to a skeptical challenge, that privacy possesses no peculiar value since its value can be explained in terms of the value we accord to other interests. According to this, conceptual clarity is served by "dissolving" privacy claims into their true components, such as property claims and claims to liberty from undue state regulation; the value of privacy can be fully explained through analyzing these components. If this challenge cannot be met, we are left with no reason to discuss the value of privacy itself. However if it can be met, we are faced with the problem of characterizing the nature of privacy's distinctive value. In particular, is privacy inherently morally undesirable, morally mixed, or desirable? Should we always flee to privacy, sometimes flee to it, or always flee from it? If we discover, as seems plausible, that privacy is correctly accorded at least a partially positive moral value, our final problem is to determine the source of this value. Do we, for example, value a woman having privacy with respect to an abortion decision because we acknowledge the dire life consequences of having an unwanted child? Or do we value privacy in such a situation because we believe that individual autonomy demands that an agent have control over a decision concerning having a child, even if it would not produce dire consequences? As these questions reveal, it is unclear whether we value privacy because it promotes desired ends, such as intimate relationships, self-respect, and freedom from the scrutiny of others, or because respecting others as autonomous agents entails according them privacy. Given the differing implications of consequentialist and deontological accounts, we must select between them in order to complete our description of privacy's normative status.

It should no longer be surprising that our everyday and legal appeals to privacy are in a state of chaos, given the multitude and diversity of responses to questions about the content, function, and value of privacy. These questions can be answered, but several steps will be necessary. We must determine whether these privacy questions are truly unresolved—have they been answered in the literature? If it provides disparate definitions, some concerned with protecting property, others with protecting personhood, should we be discussing privacy or should we reduce it to nonprivacy components? These questions constitute the focus of the first part of this book. Chapter 2 surveys the legal and philosophical literature on privacy with both a destructive and a constructive purpose; I wish to not only reveal the lack of an acceptable account of privacy, but also to introduce the key privacy debates. Chapter 3 takes on the challenge of skepticism about privacy's independent existence. I criticize the arguments of Judith Jarvis Thomson, a representative privacy skeptic, focusing on her paper "The Right to Privacy,"[6] in which she suggests that talk about the right to privacy should be abandoned since the right to privacy is merely a composite of more basic property rights and rights over the person. I believe that her claim stumbles on two points. First, assuming that the right to privacy consists of such a composite, there remains the question of which shared feature identifies these rights; a shared feature would reveal that privacy claims are at least conceptually separable from property and personhood claims as a whole. Of course, privacy claims might be conceptually separable without being normatively separable; we might accord the same value to privacy claims as we accord to property rights and rights over the person. My second point is that the value we accord to privacy does not derive necessarily from the value we accord other rights. Hence Thomson fails to establish that talk about privacy can be reduced to talk about the nature and value of other concepts without conceptual or moral loss.

Lacking a unified definition of privacy, while rejecting Thomson's contention that such a definition would serve no useful purpose, the next problem is to construct a satisfactory definition of privacy. As I have mentioned, it is necessary to determine the nature of the relation that privacy establishes between the agent and the external world. In light of this, Chapter 4 addresses the question of whether privacy works through separation or control, in other words, whether privacy merely separates particular areas of an agent's life from others or provides her with control over these areas. Although so-called privacy appeals have often been used to justify separating people and their concerns from the public realm, I suggest that privacy does not work this way. Separation-based accounts distort our privacy claims, undermining the commonly supported intuitions that underlie everyday claims. Furthermore, they fail to accord with the reasons we have for believing that privacy is a necessarily positively valued state, making it indistinguishable from such states as isolation and deprivation, turning it into only a contingent good. Control-based definitions allow us to retain our foundational privacy intuitions while accounting for privacy's necessarily positive value. They allow us to distinguish between privacy and undesirable states such as unwanted isolation. Given their explanatory power, we must reject the commonly accepted antithesis between privacy and publicity and accept that privacy provides the agent with control over a realm of her world. But what is the scope of this realm? What belongs within it—love letters, decisions about sexuality, or parking tickets?

Chapter 5 starts by noting the three central candidates for the content of privacy: control over information about oneself, access to oneself, or one's intimate decisions about one's own actions. Although privacy is usually defined in terms of only one of these categories, I suggest that its content can only be satisfactorily described in terms of all three. Privacy involves an agent controlling the information in her love letters as well as who accesses her through a kiss; privacy provides an agent with control over visual access to her naked body as well as her decisions about contraceptives. Although the categories of information, access, and decisions are individually too narrow to capture the content of privacy, they are too broad to work as a whole. Privacy cannot be invoked to protect *all* information about an agent, access to her, or decisions regarding her actions: diary information is privacy protected, but not an agent's last name; touching a woman's breasts violates her privacy, but not tapping her shoulder; decisions about autonomous sexuality are privacy protected, but not decisions about dessert. These facts are explained by Chapter 5's conclusion: privacy offers control over decisions about intimate information, intimate access, and intimate actions. The only question is, what constitutes intimacy?

Chapter 6 introduces two explanations of intimacy. We can assume that it is a feature of behavior *qua* behavior; according to this account, sexual activity is intimate because of some property of sexual behavior itself, such as its self-regarding nature. Our task is to identify the specific feature constituting intimacy. Alternatively, we can assume that intimacy is not a feature of behavior but of the motivational structure that underlies intimate activities and actions; according to this account, sexual activity is judged intimate only because we usually presuppose that certain motivations, such as love, underlie such activity. Our job is to locate the specific motivations constituting intimacy and to explain how they are tied to the intimacy of activities and actions. This chapter contends that we must reject the behavior-based characterization of intimacy because behavior is clearly not intrinsically intimate; any instance of behavior, such as kissing, might forfeit its intimacy in a different culture or historical period. When I claim that an act, such as kissing another, is intimate, I am not discussing the nature of the behavior; I am referring to the fact that the kiss expresses my affection for another. As this example reveals, intimacy claims assert that specific motivations undergird acts. In particular, I contend that to claim that an activity or action is intimate is to claim that it draws its meaning and value from the agent's love, care, or liking; intimate decisions concern such acts or activities. Furthermore, an intimacy claim asserts that something derives its significance from the agent's love, care, or liking from *her* point of view. When, for example, an individual calls her homosexual sexual activities intimate, she is claiming that they express her care, liking, or love, not that society as a whole shares this view. Hence, intimacy claims are claims about the motivations of persons, not the nature of actions, and since they embody the personal point of view, claims to control intimate decisions—that is, privacy claims—are claims to possess autonomy with respect to the expression of love, liking, and care.[7]

Privacy claims protect a realm of emotional autonomy. But why do we value this protection? Chapter 7 takes up the question of privacy's value. There are two contending explanations. First of all, privacy might derive its value from its promotion of close relationships; since the agent is in the best position to select the recipient of her love, liking, and care, close relationships are maximized by allowing individual choice. Second of all, privacy might be accorded value because it expresses our respect for persons as rational choosers; if persons are granted autonomy with respect to selecting shoes, the same principle dictates that they should possess autonomy with respect to selecting emotional partners. In this chapter, I show that both of these explanations fail, but not before they provide clues about a satisfactory account of the value of privacy. If its value were rooted in its consequentialist promotion of close relationships, privacy claims would always be contingent on the inability of others to promote an agent's relationships. However, we value privacy because of the protection it offers us against even those who could more effectively promote desired consequences; if a computer could do a better job of selecting our close relationships than we could do ourselves, this would be exactly the scenario in which we would most avidly seek privacy. Hence, we need a nonconsequentialist account. Nevertheless, we cannot explain privacy's value in terms of respect for persons as rational choosers; if we did, the value we would accord to choosing our sexual partner would be similar to the value we accord to selecting the shoes we put on in the morning. However, we value selecting our sexual partner because we are selecting the object of our affections, not merely staging an exercise in rational choice. Therefore, we need to explain privacy's value in terms of the distinctive emotions it protects. Tying together these needs, I suggest that privacy's value stems from a modified principle of respect for persons, which entails respect for them as beings with the capacity for love, care, and liking, as well as rationality. Thus, we value privacy because it embodies our respect for persons as autonomous loving, caring, and liking beings.

Since my original incentive to explore privacy stemmed from my disenchantment with the confusion of privacy law, an area of law that has been called a "haystack in a hurricane," I return to privacy law in Chapter 8 to see whether my account of privacy can impose order on this haystack.[8] I start by sketching three challenges directed at tort and constitutional privacy law. First, tort and constitutional privacy law are said to protect radically different interests, making it misleading to describe both areas of law in terms of privacy. Second, they are said to protect only an arbitrary jumble of unrelated interests, which should be abandoned for the sake of conceptual clarity. Third, the value we accord them is claimed to be indistinguishable from that which we accord liberty from undue state intervention, freedom from mental distress, and property claims; hence, all claims about the interests protected by tort and constitutional privacy should be "reduced" to discussion of interests that are protected by non-privacy areas of the law. However, an intimacy-based account of privacy avoids these challenges because intimacy is the common denominator that internally organizes and externally links tort and constitutional privacy law. Externally, intimacy is the characteristic that links them; these areas are both concerned with protecting a sphere of intimacy for the agent. Internally, intimacy is the conceptual and norma-tive core of the seemingly divergent constitutional and tort privacy rulings, which can be discovered by considering the lower courts' rulings on matters of intimate physical and informational access and the Supreme Court's rulings on matters such as contraceptive distribution, the home, abortion, and marriage.

Understanding privacy entails understanding a multitude of other matters, such as control, intimacy, personhood, and privacy law. Chapter 9 suggests that these matters are only the beginning of understanding the theoretical web in which privacy is embedded. This chapter explains how the questions originally raised by the legal and philosophical privacy literature have been resolved, yet points out that for every question resolved in this work a new question has emerged. Privacy protects love, care, and liking, but how are we to judge what truly constitutes these emotions? We respect an agent's privacy because we respect her as an emotional being, but is this respect compatible with respecting her as a rational being? If constitutional and tort privacy law are theoretically well founded, what does this suggest about the optimal growth of these areas of law?

The account of privacy in this book leads us onto paths extending far beyond privacy, paths that explore theories of human action, human nature, emotions, and the law. Thus, this work must be understood as thoughts that are yet to be embedded in an expanding web of theory. Not only are larger questions about privacy's theoretical context left unex-plored in this book, three points about privacy itself are also not examined. First, I do not consider the question of whether privacy should be described as a right or an interest; thus the validity of my arguments is not contingent on a satisfactory explanation of rights. To echo the words of Judith DeCew in her paper "The Scope of Privacy in Law and Ethics," I am making "moral and legal points which are significant independently of whether we can ultimately make sense of rights."[9] Second, my concern is with providing a definition of privacy that captures our normative use of the term, that explains what a person means when she states, "I have, possess, or experience privacy with respect to *X*." My account of privacy is not designed to explain our adjectival use of privacy's cognate, "private."[10] Finally, the following pages do not provide a transcultural and transhistorical account of privacy (if indeed such an account is even possible); my account of privacy aims at explaining the privacy claims of individuals in modern, liberal Western society. These important privacy issues lie outside of the limited scope of this book. Given these parameters, let us turn to the legal and philosophical mire of privacy theory.

Notes

1. The People of the State of Illinois v. Elizabeth H. Kohrig 113 Ill. 2d 384 (1986).

2. Bowers v. Hardwick, 85 U.S. 140 (1986).

3. For legal cases that illustrate the broad scope of privacy claims, see P. Allan Dionisopoulos and Craig Ducat, *The Right to Privacy* (St. Paul: West Publishing Co., 1976), a handbook of legal cases involving privacy.

4. The fact that some people's moral intuitions clash with the actual rulings in court cases cannot be fully explained by reference to features of adjudication unrelated to privacy, such as the judge's position on legal interpretation; the cases clearly introduce substantive disagreements about the nature and value of privacy itself.

5. After reflection, I have decided to resolve the problem of male and female pronouns by using "she" rather than "he." Although I believe that neither "she" nor "he" is a generic term, "she" has the advantage of clearly displaying its specificity. As far as my decision not to use both pronouns, the so-called generic masculine has dominated our language to such an extent that we now require affirmative action for "she." When we reach the day on which we can refer to a brain surgeon as "she" without making anyone flinch, then we will be free to use both genders for pronouns.

6. Judith Jarvis Thomson, "The Right to Privacy," *Philosophy and Public Affairs* 4 (1975): 295–314.

7. Of course, these claims take the form of claims to autonomy with respect to the actions expressing these emotions; we cannot be said to possess autonomy with respect to an emotion unless it can be expressed or not expressed in action.

8. Ettore v. Philco Television Broadcasting Co., 229 F.2d 481 (3d Cir. 1956).

9. Judith DeCew, "The Scope of Privacy in Law and Ethics," *Law and Philosophy* 5 (1986): 147.

2

Common Debates in the Philosophical and Legal Privacy Literature

Privacy is an intensely contested interest in everyday life and the law, which may explain the disorder of privacy theory. In attempting to bring order to the legal and philosophical privacy literature, we encounter two related problems. First, the content of the legal literature seems disparate from that of the philosophical literature; this leaves us wondering whether the issues at stake in tort and constitutional privacy debates are related to the conceptual debates in the philosophical literature. Second, this confusion makes it difficult to determine the parameters of debate even *within* law or philosophy, or to decide whether such parameters actually exist. However, these two worries can be resolved. Careful exploration of the privacy literature reveals that the legal and philosophical privacy debates express common concerns and that a framework for thinking about the nature and value of privacy can be constructed from them. In what follows, I show how this framework emerges and conclude with a list of questions that must be answered if we are to arrive at a unified notion of privacy.

To understand the concept of privacy, perhaps the most obvious source of potential clarification is privacy law, in which a large number of cases have been argued on the grounds of privacy. It is reasonable to suppose that both a definition and an explanation of privacy's value undergird privacy law; after all, if so many crucial legal decisions have been justified by appeal to privacy, we might imagine that there is a core of agreement about its nature and value. However, this reasonable supposition collapses upon examining privacy law. Not only does it lack a coherent definition of privacy and account of its value, it also lacks agreement on whether such a claim is conceptually and morally separable from others.

Privacy law consists of both tort and constitutional privacy law. Tort privacy law focuses on the damage an individual can sustain due to unwanted access from others. This access may take the form of the unwanted distribution, gathering, or attempted gathering of information about an agent; it may also take the form of gaining noninformational access to an agent. As William Prosser notes, tort privacy law offers protection against a variety of harms: "intrusion upon the plaintiff's seclusion or solitude, or into his private affairs, public disclosure of embarrassing private facts about the plaintiff, publicity which places the plaintiff in a false light in the public eye, and appropriation, for the defendant's advantage, of the plaintiff's name or likeness."[1] The type of protection tort privacy law offers against these intrusions can be described as a "right to be left alone" with respect to various forms of access by others.[2] In other words, it enforces an agent's claim to have physical and informational access to herself restricted.

As it has developed since 1965, the independent constitutional right to privacy is not chiefly concerned with restricting the access of others to the agent.[3] Rather, it focuses on the harm an agent can sustain if her liberty with respect to her own intimate actions is undermined. Hence, constitutional privacy law protects the agent by according her a realm of autonomy with respect to decisions about those actions. These decisions involve such diverse matters as marriage, procreation, family relations, abortion, child rearing, and the home.[4] More generally, constitutional privacy protects the agent's freedom of action in what is aptly termed "the private sphere"—the sphere of the home, sexuality, the body, and the family. Given this sketch of privacy law, let us consider why we cannot successfully understand privacy simply through referring to tort or constitutional privacy law.

The first problem legal privacy theory faces is that it fails to agree upon even whether privacy is conceptually separable from other claims. On the one hand, the vast body of legal cases and papers that discuss privacy attests to the fact that many jurists believe an independent legal claim to it exists that cannot be reduced to claims about other interests. On the other hand, legal reductionists advance a skeptical claim, arguing that privacy is not conceptually distinct and should be abandoned for the sake of conceptual clarity. For example, William Prosser suggests that tort privacy "is a complex of four distinct . . . torts."[5] Harry Kalven states that "privacy seems a less precise way of approaching more specific values, as, for example, in the case of freedom of speech, association, and religion."[6] Similarly, Justice Rehnquist explains that "a group of quite separate and different values that have been assembled under the heading of 'privacy' could be more meaningfully evaluated if they were more accurately cataloged."[7] Though this reductionist skepticism about privacy is not logically tied to the rift between tort and constitutional privacy law, in reality the rift has contributed much support to the skeptical position. Given the apparently disparate areas of life enclosed within constitutional and tort privacy, legal theorists claim that this split reflects the "fact" that the concept of privacy lacks conceptual distinctness. These skeptical claims and nonskeptical counterclaims splinter privacy law, making it impossible for us to readily determine even whether an independent legal interest in privacy exists.

The second reason privacy law fails to produce an unified account of privacy is that tort and constitutional law generate different, seemingly incompatible, definitions of privacy. Tort law defines it as the state of an agent having personal information or experience separated from the senses of others. Hence, tort privacy law is concerned with separating the agent from the access of others. Yet constitutional law defines privacy as the state of an agent having control over her decisions insofar as they refer to her own intimate actions. Hence, constitutional law is primarily concerned with protecting the agent's freedom of intimate action. These definitions are not merely superficially different: they are based on differing accounts of both the function and content of privacy. According to tort law, privacy functions through separation; since an agent can be separated from the senses of others without having control over the separation, the state of privacy does not necessarily entail control. Yet constitutional law provides a control-based account of privacy; since an agent can have control without separation from others, the state of privacy does not necessarily entail separation. As for the content of privacy, tort law suggests that it covers access to the individual (either to information about her or to her experiences). Yet, according to constitutional law, the content of privacy covers intimate decisions about actions, not matters of access. Given these different accounts of the function and content of privacy, which give rise to different definitions, our problem emerges. We cannot accept both definitions as it appears that they differ on a fundamental level, yet we cannot abandon either, since they both plausibly claim to define privacy.

Not only is privacy law torn by disagreements about privacy's conceptual distinctness and definition, it is also beset with disagreements about its value. The legal debates focus on two central questions. First of all, does privacy have any value peculiar to itself; for example, is the value we accord to it different from the value we accord to liberty from undue state intervention? Should we be talking about the value of privacy in the first place? This debate about privacy's independent normative identity is the natural extension of the debate between the skeptics and nonskeptics about its independent conceptual identity.[8] Second of all, is privacy's value best described in consequentialist or deontological terms? Case law mentions that privacy is valuable for such diverse purposes as "promotion of free discourse," "to secure conditions favorable to the pursuit of happiness," "leading lives in health and safety" in the home, "to keep secret or intimate facts about oneself from the prying eyes or ears of others," and the promotion of personal relationships.[9] With claims such as these, the courts suggest that privacy is valuable because of its desirable consequences. Yet there is also a deontological strand in legal privacy theory. The law contains suggestions that privacy's value stems from respect for "man's spiritual nature," "individual dignity," and "inviolate personality."[10] Since a consequentialist account of privacy's value will ultimately clash with a deontological account, we must arbitrate between them if we decide that privacy does possess an independent value.

As we have seen, the legal literature lacks a unified account of privacy's nature and value; we cannot resolve its chaotic state simply through recourse to privacy law. But what about the philosophical literature? In what follows, I show that, although characterized by wideranging disagreements, it addresses a few central issues that parallel those found in the legal discussions about privacy. This gives us grounds to hope that these key questions can be used as a framework around which we can organize the privacy intuitions of ordinary life, the law, and philosophy.[11]

Philosophers are in no more agreement about the conceptual distinctness of privacy than are jurists. On the one hand, there are the skeptics. As was the case in the law, these skeptics argue that privacy claims can be reduced to claims about other human interests with no conceptual loss; for example, Judith Jarvis Thomson contends that the concept of privacy lacks a common core and that our privacy claims can be expressed both more directly and clearly if they are reduced to their true constituents: property interests and interests in controlling our physical bodies.[12] Similarly, H. J. McCloskey argues that the study of privacy is not fruitful on the grounds that "any right to privacy will be a derivative one from other rights and other goods."[13] On the other hand, a vast body of philosophical literature attempts to provide an account that cannot be reduced to nonprivacy interests, thus either tacitly or explicitly denying the skeptics' claim. For example, James Rachels argues that privacy claims have "a different *point*" from other claims and should not be expected to overlap with them; furthermore, even assuming this overlap, he contends that privacy is still "a distinctive sort of right in virtue of the special kind of interest it protects."[14]

The legal disagreements concerning the definition of privacy focused on the apparent incompatibility of the definition based on tort law (the state of the agent's inaccessibility) with the definition underlying constitutional law (the state of the agent's control over certain intimate decisions about her own actions). The debates in the philosophical literature are rooted in the same fundamental problems about the function of privacy and its content.

Philosophers debate how privacy works, centering on whether privacy functions through a mechanism of control or through restricting access to the agent. For example, Anita Allen, Roland Garrett, Ruth Gavison, William Parent, and Hyman Gross contend that restricted access is at the core of privacy.[15] According to them, to claim that a person experiences privacy logically entails that some aspect of her life is not accessed by others; the identifying criterion of privacy is inaccessibility. Yet Jeffrey Reiman, James Rachels, Elizabeth Beardsley, Robert Gerstein, and Richard Wasserstrom reject that idea,[16] defining privacy as the measure of control an agent possesses over a realm of her life.[17]

Philosophers also lack an unified account of the content of privacy. The literature fields two main candidates: first, privacy might regulate an agent's intimate decisions about her own actions; second, privacy might regulate access to the agent. The philosophers who choose access can be split into two groups: those who argue that privacy's scope covers only informational access to the agent and those who contend that privacy covers a variety of forms of access (without regard for whether information is actually gained from the access). For example, William Parent, Elizabeth Beardsley, Robert Gerstein, and Richard Wasserstrom all implicitly or explicitly place the regulation of information at the heart of their definitions.[18] Anita Allen, James Rachels, Jeffrey Reiman, Roland Garrett, Joseph Kupfer, Ernest Van Den Haag, and Thomas Scanlon reject this narrow interpretation of privacy as strictly informational in content, opting instead for definitions of privacy based on noninformational access.[19] As Anita Allen points out, "seclusion, anonymity, and other non-informational forms of privacy are still aims of the privacy quests of men and women."[20]

Though the above two groups of theorists are not in perfect agreement about the content of privacy, they at least share the common assumption that it is exhausted by matters of access to the agent. This assumption is not shared by Judith DeCew, Ferdinand Schoeman, Kent Greenawalt, and Tom Gerety,[21] who believe privacy regulates certain decisions an agent makes about her own actions, decisions often termed "personal" or "intimate." As Judith DeCew notes, "a subset of autonomy cases, certain personal decisions regarding one's basic lifestyle, can plausibly be said to involve privacy interests as well . . . privacy is at stake because of the *nature* of the decision."[22] These decisions, involving choices about contraception, reproduction, familial issues, and marital matters, clearly *may* regulate access to the agent, but they also involve far more. Hence, they cannot be fully explained by access-based accounts of privacy's content.

These disagreements cannot be merely dismissed as trivial or peripheral to our central task of understanding privacy. Characterizing the function of privacy in terms of control or restricted access has ramifications for both the situations we identify as involving privacy and the normative value we accord privacy. Similarly, describing privacy's content in terms of information, access, or intimate decisions about one's actions obviously changes the scope of privacy claims and has the potential to change its value. Furthermore, these problems cannot be avoided by arguing that these disagreements collapse into one another. We have no clear reason to believe that control-based definitions of privacy can be reconciled with separation-based ones, or that explanations of the content of privacy in terms of access can be reconciled with those in terms of the agent's intimate decisions about her own actions.[23]

There remains one final question to ask of the philosophical literature on privacy: does it contain a consensus on the normative value of privacy and the source of this value? Given the philosophical literature's lack of consensus with respect to the definition of privacy, it is not surprising that it lacks a unitary account of privacy's value. More interestingly, although philosophical discussion of the value of privacy is much more thorough than that found in case law, it ultimately ends up enmeshed in disagreements similar to those found in the legal literature about whether privacy possesses a unique value and, if so, the source of this value.

The theorists who argue for the "epistemological reduction" of privacy claims to those about other human interests are often also "moral reductionists" (though the two positions are not necessarily intertwined). They argue that the moral interests protected by privacy are neither coincident nor connected, thus privacy claims can be reduced to claims about other interests without the loss of anything of moral importance; for example, Judith Jarvis Thomson claims that "the wrongness of every violation of the right to privacy can be explained without ever once mentioning it."[24] Similarly, H. J. McCloskey states that "any right to privacy will be a derivative one from other rights and other goods."[25] Furthermore, value skeptics such as Thomson and McCloskey not only see moral reductionism as a *possible* task, but also a desirable one— moral clarity is preserved by focusing on the value of the primary interests from which the composite value of privacy is derived. However, the majority of privacy theorists reject the reductionist route; for example, Jeffrey Reiman and James Rachels contend that something special about privacy's moral character is abandoned by the reductionists.[26] Reiman explains that "there is indeed something unique protected by the right to privacy. . . . And if we miss it, there may come a time when we think we are merely limiting some personal or property right in favor of some greater good, when in fact we are really sacrificing something of much greater value."[27] Similarly, Rachels argues that reductionist "dissociation separates this right [the right to privacy] from the matters that make *privacy* important."[28] This debate between the moral reductionists and their opponents clearly cannot be bypassed: privacy cannot lack *and* possess a distinctive value at the same time.

The disagreements continue among the philosophers who accept that privacy has an unique value. The disagreement found in case law concerning whether privacy's value stems from its consequences or a principle of respect for persons extends into the philosophical literature, though with new twists. Rather than merely listing the goals promoted by privacy, such as unconstrained discourse or happiness in the home, the consequentialist philosophical literature attempts to unify these consequences. This depends upon a consequential link between privacy and relationships. James Rachels, Robert Gerstein, and Charles Fried suggest that privacy is valuable because certain relationships cannot be established between individuals without privacy.[29] As Rachels explains, "if we cannot control who has access to us, sometimes including and sometimes excluding various people, then we cannot control the patterns of behavior we need to adopt . . . or the kinds of relations with other people that we will have."[30] Similarly, Gerstein links the value of privacy to its promotion of intimate relationships.[31] Since these philosophers assume that the creation and promotion of relationships have moral value, they conclude that the value of privacy flows from this consequence.[32]

Stanley Benn, Jeffrey Reiman, Ferdinand Schoeman, and Joseph Kupfer contend that privacy's value is rooted in respect for moral personhood.[33] As Benn explains after rejecting a consequentialist account of privacy's value, "It was not that allowing men privacy would give them a better chance to be autonomous. It was rather that a person—anyone potentially autonomous—was worthy of respect on that account; and that if such a person wished to pursue his enterprise unobserved, he was entitled".[34] According to this argument, moral persons are fundamentally rational choosers. If they are to be respected as persons, this capacity must be respected. Privacy is valued because it embodies our respect for persons as choosers. Failing to accord an agent privacy may or may not curtail her goals, but this is not the core of the harm: the core of the harm is that her status as a moral person has been violated.

This final conflict between an explanation of privacy's value in terms of the close relationships it promotes and in terms of respect for personhood cannot be resolved in any straightforward manner. Neither of these accounts is clearly misguided, but we cannot accept both of them as accurate since they have different implications for our actions. If privacy's value lay in its promotion of close relationships, it would be perfectly justifiable to deny an individual's privacy if a more effective route were discovered; yet explaining privacy's value in terms of respect for persons would undermine our justification for such a paternalistic action. Thus, we are trapped in the quandary we have previously encountered—the philosophical literature on privacy contains a fundamental disagreement about its value.

Although case law and philosophy lack a commonly accepted definition of privacy and explanation of its moral value, the previous pages fulfill not only the negative task of determining the demands that the literature *cannot* satisfy. If we focus on the commonalities between the debates in case law and the philosophical literature, we discover the positive result of this chapter: these commonalities provide shape and content to questions about privacy's nature and value, a starting point for an account of privacy.

The debates shared between the legal and philosophical literature can be grouped into three categories: (1) the skeptical debate about the conceptual and moral distinctness of privacy; (2) the debate about the two components of a definition of privacy—the function of privacy and the content of privacy; (3) the debate about the value of privacy.

The skeptical debate centers on two questions: Is privacy a conceptually distinct concept? Is a claim to privacy morally distinct?[35] There is both a reductionist and nonreductionist response to these questions. Reductionists have a prescriptive and descriptive argument. On the descriptive side, they argue that privacy claims can be expressed in terms of claims about more fundamental human interests with neither conceptual nor moral loss. On the prescriptive side, they contend that privacy claims should be reduced in this manner for the sake of conceptual and normative clarity. Nonreductionists contend that privacy is both conceptually and morally distinct. Given these questions and responses, the first step in constructing an adequate account of privacy is to determine whether the moral or conceptual distinctness of privacy can be established in such a way as to respond to reductionist concerns.

The debate concerning the definition of privacy also focuses on two questions. How does privacy function? What is the content of privacy? The privacy literature contains two explanations. Privacy may work by separating a realm of the agent's life from the access of others, or it may work by providing the agent with control over a realm of her life. With regard to the content of privacy, the literature suggests that privacy covers either an agent's intimate decisions about her own actions, informational access to her, or general access to her. Hence, in creating a satisfactory account of privacy, we must define it in light of these questions. This task involves two steps: explaining whether privacy functions through control or separation, then characterizing privacy's content in terms of intimate decisions, information, or access.

The final debate I wish to draw out from the legal and philosophical literature focuses on the source of privacy's value. The privacy literature offers two possible sources. First of all, privacy may be valued because it promotes the desired consequence of close relationships between people.

Second of all, privacy may be valued because we respect persons as choosers. Thus in developing an adequate account of privacy we must determine whether privacy's value stems from consequentialist or deontological considerations.

Notes

1. William Prosser, "Privacy [A Legal Analysis]," in *Philosophical Dimensions of Privacy,* ed. Ferdinand Schoeman (New York: Cambridge University Press, 1984), 107.

2. This characterization is often found in the tort privacy law literature. See, for example, Union Pacific Railway Co. v. Botsford, 141 U.S. 250 (1981). See also P. Allan Dionisopoulos and Craig Ducat, *The Right to Privacy* (St. Paul: West Publishing Co., 1976), 21.

3. This is not to say that questions of access have not been mentioned in constitutional privacy cases since 1965. The Court has often shown concern about what the state would have to do to obtain the access necessary to enforce the disputed law; for example in Griswold, the Court is clearly concerned that the state would have to violate the marital bedroom in order to determine whether illegal contraceptive use was taking place. See Griswold v. Connecticut, 381 U.S. 479 (1965). However, such access concerns are peripheral to the Court's central concern to provide autonomy with respect to intimate decisions. As David A. J. Richards puts it, "there is no evidence that the constitutional right to privacy depends on outrageous government surveillance violative of conventional right-to-privacy interests"; see David A. J. Richards, "The Jurisprudence of Privacy as a Constitutional Right," in *Privacy,* ed. William Bier (New York: Fordham University Press, 1980), 139.

4. See, respectively, Loving v. Virginia, 388 U.S. 1 (1967); Griswold v. Connecticut; Carey v. Population Services International, 431 U.S. 678, 685 (1977); Roe v. Wade, 410 U.S. 113 (1973); Stanley v. Georgia, 394 U.S. 557 (1969).

5. Prosser, "Privacy [A Legal Analysis]," 124.

6. Harry Kalven, "Privacy in Tort Law: Were Warren and Brandeis Wrong?" 31 *Law and Contemporary Problems* 326 (1966): 327.

7. William H. Rehnquist, "Is an Expanded Right to Privacy Consistent with Fair and Effective Law Enforcement?" 23 *Kansas Law Review* 1 (1974).

8. In other words, assuming that privacy is conceptually distinct, there is a separate question about whether it is morally distinct. For example, the set of property claims about green objects is conceptually distinct from the set of

property claims as a whole, but this does not entail that the set of green object property claims is morally distinct from property claims in general.

9. See, respectively, United States v. White, 401 U.S. 745 (1971); Olmstead v. United States, 277 U.S. 438 (1928); Martin v. City of Struthers, 319 U.S. 141 (1943); Nader v. General Motors Corp., 25 N.Y. 2d 560 (1970); and Griswold v. Connecticut.

10. See, respectively, Olmstead v. United States, 277 U.S. 438 (1928); United States v. White; Edward Bloustein, "Privacy as an Aspect of Human Dignity: An Answer to Dean Prosser," in *Philosophical Dimensions of Privacy,* ed. Ferdinand Schoeman (New York: Cambridge University Press, 1984), 156–202.

11. A critic might contend that I cannot justifiably appeal to our "privacy intuitions" given my previous claims about the strife-ridden nature of these intuitions. Nevertheless, I hope to show that a core of shared privacy intuitions can indeed be identified.

12. See, in general, Judith Jarvis Thomson, "The Right to Privacy," *Philosophy and Public Affairs* 4 (1975): 295–314.

13. H. J. McCloskey, "Privacy and the Right to Privacy," *Philosophy* 55 (1980): 37.

14. James Rachels, "Why Privacy Is Important," *Philosophy and Public Affairs* 4 (1975): 333.

15. See, respectively, Anita Allen, *Uneasy Access: Privacy for Women in a Free Society* (New Jersey: Rowman and Littlefield, 1988); Roland Garrett, "The Nature of Privacy," *Philosophy Today* 89 (1974): 421–72; Ruth Gavison, "Privacy and the Limits of the Law," *Yale Law Journal* 89 (1980): 421–71; William A. Parent, "Recent Work on the Concept of Privacy," *American Philosophical Quarterly* 20 (1983): 341–54; Hyman Gross, "Privacy and Autonomy," in *Privacy: Nomos XIII,* ed. J. Roland Pennock and John W. Chapman (New York: Atherton Press, 1971): 169–81.

16. Jeffrey Reiman, "Privacy, Intimacy and Personhood," *Philosophy and Public Affairs* 6 (1976): 26–44; Rachels, "Why Privacy Is Important," 323–33; Elizabeth Beardsley, "Privacy: Autonomy and Self-Disclosure," in *Privacy: Nomos XIII,* ed. J. Roland Pennock and John W. Chapman (New York: Atherton Press, 1971): 56–70; Robert Gerstein, "Intimacy and Privacy," *Ethics* 89 (1978): 86–91; Richard Wasserstrom, "Privacy: Some Arguments and Assumptions," in *Philosophical Law,* ed. Richard Bronaugh (Westport, CT: Greenwood Press, 1978): 148–66.

17. Thus making inaccessibility only a *possible* manifestation of privacy; inaccessibility *may* be a manifestation of control, but it is not a logical entailment of privacy.

18. See Parent, "Recent Work on the Concept of Privacy"; Beardsley,

"Privacy: Autonomy and Self-Disclosure;" Gerstein, "Intimacy and Privacy";
Wasserstrom, "Privacy: Some Arguments and Assumptions."

19. Allen, *Uneasy Access;* Rachels, "Why Privacy Is Important"; Reiman,
"Privacy, Intimacy and Personhood"; Roland Garrett, "The Nature of Pri-
vacy," *Philosophy Today* 18 (1974): 263–84; Joseph Kupfer, "Privacy, Auton-
omy and Self-Concept," *American Philosophical Quarterly* 24 (1987): 81–88;
Ernest Van Den Haag, "On Privacy," in *Privacy: Nomos XIII,* ed. J. Roland
Pennock and John W. Chapman (New York: Atherton Press, 1971), 149–68;
Thomas Scanlon, "Thomson on Privacy," *Philosophy and Public Affairs* 4
(1975): 315–22.

20. Allen, *Uneasy Access,* 8.

21. Judith DeCew, "The Scope of Privacy in Law and Ethics," *Law and
Philosophy* 5 (1986): 145–73; Ferdinand Schoeman, "Privacy and Intimate
Information," in *Philosophical Dimensions of Privacy,* ed. Ferdinand Schoeman
(New York: Cambridge University Press, 1984), 403–18; Kent Greenawalt,
"Privacy and Its Legal Protection," *Hastings Center Studies* 2 (1974): 45–68;
Tom Gerety, "Redefining Privacy," *Harvard Civil Rights—Civil Liberties Law
Review* 12 (1977): 233–96.

22. DeCew, "The Scope of Privacy in Law and Ethics," 165.

23. This is not to suggest that it is logically impossible to discover a way to
collapse these apparently separate categories, but to make the weaker claim that
this move cannot be made in any obvious way.

24. Thomson, "The Right to Privacy," 313.

25. McCloskey, "Privacy and the Right to Privacy," 37.

26. Reiman, "Privacy, Intimacy and Personhood," 28; Rachels, "Why
Privacy Is Important," 332.

27. Reiman, "Privacy, Intimacy and Personhood," 28.

28. Rachels, "Why Privacy Is Important," 332.

29. Rachels, "Why Privacy Is Important"; Gerstein, "Intimacy and Privacy"; Charles Fried, *An Anatomy of Values* (Cambridge, MA: Harvard University Press, 1970).

30. Rachels, "Why Privacy Is Important," 331.

31. See Gerstein, "Privacy and Intimacy."

32. Of course, there is no reason why an account of privacy's value in terms of
the value of relationships *must* be consequentialist; for example, a principle of
respect for persons might dictate that one allow an agent autonomy with respect to
her relationships. All I intend to suggest in this paragraph is that there is an
important body of philosophical privacy literature that does treat the link between
privacy's value and relationships as a consequentialist one.

33. Stanley Benn, "Privacy, Freedom, and Respect for Persons," in *Privacy:
Nomos XIII,* ed. J. Roland Pennock and John W. Chapman (New York: Atherton
Press, 1971), 1–26; Reiman, "Privacy, Intimacy and Personhood"; Schoeman,

"Privacy and Intimate Information"; Kupfer, "Privacy, Autonomy and Self-Concept."

34. Benn, "Privacy, Freedom, and Respect for Persons," 26.

35. To accord with the organization of future chapters, I place questions about both privacy's conceptual and moral distinctness within the skeptical debate, despite the fact that the moral distinctness questions were initially discussed under the heading of privacy's value.

3

The Threatened Downfall of Privacy: Judith Jarvis Thomson's "The Right to Privacy" and Skepticism about Privacy

Do we have any reason to believe that the claims assembled under the heading "privacy" are conceptually and morally coherent, or are they simply a jumble of disparate claims and their heterogeneous normative values, which should be abandoned for the sake of clarity? Although the answer may appear obvious—ordinary and legal discourse constantly imply that privacy claims do have a distinct meaning and value—certain philosophers and legal scholars have rejected this response. Instead, these skeptics argue that the meaning and value accorded to privacy claims are irreducibly heterogeneous, since privacy is merely a composite of unrelated elements, such as property interests and interests in self-ownership. Hence, talk about privacy should be "reduced" to talk about its disparate elements to avoid suggesting that there is something distinct about it—the concept itself needs no special investigation. The task of this chapter is to adjudicate between these two responses before presenting my positive account of privacy. As the burden of proof clearly lies on the skeptic's side, I first consider the arguments contained in a paper encapsulating the skeptical criticisms of privacy—Judith Jarvis Thomson's "The Right to Privacy."[1]

In "The Right to Privacy," Thomson argues that the right to privacy is inherently unclear because it lacks a unitary conceptual and normative core, despite our intuitions to the contrary.[2] She suggests that all discussion about privacy should be "reduced" to a discussion of other rights, specifically property rights and rights over the person. This reduction requires her to establish three interlocking points. First of all, she must show that privacy rights can be expressed in terms of other rights. Second of all, she needs to demonstrate that privacy rights are secondary rights derived from these primary nonprivacy rights. Finally, she must establish that deriving privacy rights from other rights entails that appeals to privacy rights *should* be abandoned—their abandonment yields a loss of neither meaning nor value. In what follows, I discuss Thomson's arguments for these points and show that she fails to establish the possibility or desirability of her reductionist program.

Given that Thomson's task is to reduce the right to privacy to other rights, let us first consider what constitutes privacy for her. Thomson never explicitly defines privacy in "The Right to Privacy," perhaps due to her belief that even a seemingly unified definition would undermine her contention that the right to privacy is not properly understood as unified.[3] However, she does provide an array of examples of privacy violations from which we can extract an implicit account. This account has two parts. First, Thomson works with a restricted-access account of privacy. An agent has privacy to the extent that a realm of her life is not accessed by others, hence, the right to privacy is a right not to be accessed. Second, Thomson includes two aspects of life within the scope of privacy. Privacy involves restricting access through such senses as touch, sight, and hearing to certain objects in the external world, notably our material possessions (although Thomson seems to be most concerned with restricting access via sight).[4] Privacy also involves restricting access through the senses to our bodies (although Thomson only explicitly considers sight and hearing).[5] Therefore, the right to privacy is a right to restrict another's access to our possessions and person. Thomson's view is illustrated by her primary examples of uncontested privacy violations, one of which involves a pornographic picture and another a fight. In the pornographic picture example, she considers the dire situation of a man who owns a pornographic picture.

> He wants that nobody but him shall ever see that picture—perhaps because he wants that nobody shall know that he owns it, perhaps because he feels that someone else's seeing it would drain it of power to please. So he keeps it locked in his wall-safe, and takes it out to look at only at night or after pulling down the shades. . . . We have heard about his picture, and we

want to see it, so we train our X-ray device on the wall-safe and look in. To do this is, I think, to violate a right of his—the right to privacy, I should think.[6]

In this example, the violation of privacy stems from the fact that another has achieved visual access to a possession—the pornographic picture. Thomson's second example of a privacy violation reveals that privacy violations need not involve material possessions: "If my husband and I are having a quiet fight behind closed windows and cannot be heard by the normal person who passes by, then if anyone trains an amplifier on us in order to listen he violates a right, the right to privacy, in fact."[7] In this example, the violation of privacy results from another's aural access to the voice of the disputants—an aspect of their person.

Assuming that the rights clustered under the right to privacy involve rights to restrict access to both our possessions and person, we can seek to understand privacy in one of two ways: by seeking similarity or dissimilarity in this cluster. We can attempt to discover why cases involving access to possessions and those involving access to the person are both said to involve privacy, or we can accentuate the differences between access to possessions and to the person. Thomson does not argue for some inherent similarity between the case involving the pornographic picture and the case involving the overheard argument. Instead, she looks at these situations and sees only dissimilarity, arguing that the pornographic picture case involves a violation of property rights, while the fight case involves a violation of rights over the person. From these specific cases, Thomson derives a general characterization of the twofold nature of privacy claims: privacy-protected access to objects in the external world stems from property rights, while privacy-protected access to the person stems from rights over the person.

We commonly think of property rights as the right to sell possessions and the right that others not sell those possessions without permission. On the surface, property rights do not explicitly include such privacy rights as the right not to have a pornographic picture examined. More generally, it is not immediately obvious that ownership rights entail any privacy claims, claims involving restricting another's "sensing" of possessions. Thomson views this intuitive separation between property and privacy claims as a product to carelessness or conceptual confusion. According to her, privacy claims to restrict access to something in the external world amount to nothing more than property rights. For example, she argues that not only do we possess commonly accepted property rights with respect to the pornographic picture, we also have the less-discussed property right that others shall not look at the picture; the owner of the picture may justifiably conceal it due to the rights granted to him by ownership. When another violates this property right by looking at the picture, the violation stems from the fact that the picture possessor's ownership interests are violated; this violation can be explained without any reference to privacy. Furthermore, the privacy right to regulate visual access to something is not merely accompanied by ownership claims, but is inseparable from ownership. Objects that are not owned, such as a subway map, do not give rise to justified privacy claims. Ownership is both a necessary and sufficient condition for having a privacy right not to have some object in the external world accessed by the senses of others.

Thomson views the privacy interests in the overheard argument case as similar to those involved in the pornographic picture case. She admits that "we do not . . . care nearly as much about our possessions as we care about ourselves."[8] Yet she goes on to claim that this fact merely provides us with more stringent rights with respect to our persons than with respect to our possessions, not with an entirely different kind of right. Thomson suggests that these more stringent rights over the person include many "un-grand" rights not commonly mentioned in philosophical debate, including such diverse rights as the right not to have our elbows painted green and the right not to have our hair cut off while we sleep.[9] As far as privacy is concerned, the core group of un-grand personhood rights that are also privacy rights consist of the agent's various rights not to be accessed via another's senses, especially the agent's right to be neither looked at nor listened to. The reason we have the right to limit access to our persons is that we are limiting access to our *own* bodies and voices; bodily "ownership" generates a right to limit access in the same way ownership of possessions entails a right to limit access. Hence, in the case of the amplified argument, the violation of privacy stems from the violation of bodily ownership rights. The involved parties had their privacy violated *just because* they had their "property" (their voices) accessed; the violation does not lie in the content of the vocal "property" that was expropriated.

After having argued that all privacy claims involve property claims or claims about self-ownership, Thomson goes on to argue that privacy claims hold a conceptually and normatively secondary, derivative position, with property rights and rights over the person holding the primary position. To establish this conclusion, she starts by noting that the right to privacy is a melange of property rights and rights over the person that lacks a distinctive conceptual focus. She combines this observation with the "simplifying hypothesis" that privacy rights can be explained without even mentioning the right to privacy itself.[10] Therefore, the right to privacy can be conceptually "simplified" out of existence because every privacy right can be fully explained in terms of the property right or right over the person from which it is derived. The right to privacy does not stand on the same footing as property rights and rights over the person, but rather exists only as a conceptually secondary right cluster that has been derived from these primary right clusters. Furthermore, the right to privacy is also vulnerable to normative simplification; the moral wrong of privacy violations can be explained in terms of the moral wrong attendant upon violating the primary rights that give rise to the right to privacy. Because she believes that the conceptual and normative signifi-cance of privacy can be explained in terms of other rights, Thomson concludes that we *should* abandon discussion of privacy—our quixotic quest for privacy's conceptual and normative core is bound to be fruitless. Our confusion about the nature of privacy is best dispelled by abandoning theorizing about the right to privacy and retreating to the confines of property rights and rights over the person, wherein we can discover the interests that actually lie concealed under the blanket "right to privacy." When faced with a situation involving an apparent indepen-dent privacy claim, the situation is simply mystified by seeking to isolate a distinct privacy right.

Thomson's attempt to reduce the right to privacy into fragments of property rights and rights over the person is an interesting maneuver. If it were successful, she would have established not only the misguided nature of many philosophical attempts to come to terms with privacy, but also the flawed nature of our basic intuition that privacy claims have a distinct meaning and value. But is her argument successful? In what follows, I argue that the concept of privacy proves remarkably resilient to Thomson's attack. I start by raising some questions about her claim for the derivative status of privacy rights, especially with respect to their derivation from property rights and rights over the person. I then argue that, even allowing her derivative argument to stand, we are not neces-sarily forced to accept her conclusion that there is no need to explore any further the rights contained in the privacy cluster.

Let me first point out that Thomson's account of privacy is at the very least partially correct. It is undeniable that accessing another's possessions or person *can* constitute a privacy violation; for example, looking at another's love letters or grabbing her breast without permission clearly constitute privacy violations. Thus, what follows does not criticize the idea that issues concerning property or the person *can* be included under privacy rights, but calls into question whether privacy rights simply *are* property rights and rights over the person.

As I have previously mentioned, the first point Thomson has to establish is that all privacy claims can be expressed in terms of non-privacy claims, which she attempts to do by arguing that all privacy claims with regard to objects in the external world invoke property rights, while all privacy claims with respect to the person invoke self-ownership rights. However, I suggest that having a justified property claim or self-ownership claim is neither a necessary nor a sufficient condition for having a justified privacy claim, giving us no reason to see privacy claims as necessarily related to such ownership claims. Let us first consider this argument with respect to privacy and objects in the external world.

Thomson argues that privacy claims about objects in the external world amount to property claims. Unfortunately for her argument, privacy claims about such objects often extend beyond property claims while not necessarily failing as privacy claims, which suggests that such privacy claims do not amount to proclaiming, "It's mine!" Privacy rights appear to adhere to personal objects even when property rights have been relinquished. To illustrate this, imagine that I have written a number of love letters to another person. By sending these letters to the person, I relinquish possession of them, yet although the letters are no longer mine, my privacy is still violated if my lover copies the letters and distributes them to others without my consent.[11] In this case, my claim to privacy with respect to the love letters can be disconnected from ownership, the claim continuing to have a foundation even when my ownership rights have been relinquished (although we could clearly argue about the strength of the claim).[12] Hence, privacy claims can attach to objects in the absence of property claims.

Privacy claims not only extend beyond property claims in various cases, they also seem to stop short of property claims in other situations, in other words, justified property claims do not necessarily entail justified privacy claims. In particular, the fact that nonintimate possessions are *mine* does not suggest that my privacy claims with respect to those possessions are necessarily justified.[13] For example, if a friend examines my pen sitting on my desk, she usually does not violate my privacy despite the fact that it is *my* pen, but if she examines my open diary on the desk, a privacy violation occurs. In the first case, a privacy claim on my part would be unreasonable (despite my property claim). If I made such a claim, perhaps telling my friend, "You violated my privacy—it's *my* pen!," she would not question the fact of my ownership; rather, she would point out, "It's only a pen!" In the second case, I have grounds for both a property and privacy claim. As this example illustrates, only certain sorts of property are accompanied by privacy claims; privacy claims are not indiscriminately attached to the simple fact of ownership.[14]

A similar problem emerges when we consider the relationship between privacy claims involving access to an agent's self and claims of self-ownership (in Thomson's terminology, rights over the person). Once again, privacy rights over the person may often overlap bodily "possession rights," but this is not always the case. Privacy rights involving access to the self extend beyond the realm of self-ownership; we can make justified privacy claims even in the absence of justified self-ownership claims. For example, if I were seated on a bus, indulging in an innocent (though quiet) conversation with a friend, and a stranger on the bus suddenly stuck her head between our heads in a blatant attempt to hear the conversation, my privacy would be violated even if the stranger heard nothing because of the abrupt cessation of the conversation due to the intrusion. Similarly, if I were on a train with closed compartments, and I noticed someone sneaking up to take a look at me, my privacy would be violated even if I managed to hide under the bed before the person actually saw me. In neither of these two scenarios has my "possession" of my voice or image been damaged—I cannot claim that my Thomsonian self-ownership rights have been violated. Despite this, I can justifiably contend that my privacy has been violated. This suggests that privacy rights concerning access to the person cannot be collapsed into bodily ownership claims, but form a zone that extends beyond the zone of ownership.[15]

Privacy rights also stop short of possession rights over the person. Possession rights over nonintimate aspects of the person (body, voice, etc.) do not necessarily give rise to privacy rights; for example, if my friend came to the door of my house and, in pausing to think for a moment before ringing the doorbell, heard me say "the," I would not have grounds on which to claim a privacy violation. But if that same friend stood in front of my door for hours, straining to hear my quiet conversation inside, my privacy would be violated (assuming I had not given her permission to listen). Similarly, if a person on the street glanced at me momentarily through my open window on the street, I would lack grounds for a privacy violation claim. Yet if that same person stared in my window throughout the entire day, my privacy would be violated. In these cases, the agent's voice and image *have* been successfully appropriated; if there is indeed such a thing as a Thomsonian ownership right to an agent's voice and image, this has been violated. But the impersonality of the access gained in the first of these pairs of cases precludes justified privacy claims.

Of course, Thomson could respond by claiming that the right to privacy was waived in the situations that do not seem to be obvious privacy violations, but how have I waived my privacy in those instances but not in the other ones? My behavior has remained the same, while the other's changes, but it is *I* who have waived my Thomsonian right. She could also argue that a nonwaived right to privacy exists in both cases, the difference being that I hold the right to privacy as less stringent in certain situations. This move would require two things. She would have to establish the existence of a right not to have, for example, a friend hear me say "the" while standing at my doorbell, countering the obvious intuition that this case does not involve even a trivial privacy violation. She would also need to address the question of why our privacy rights attach with more stringency in certain cases—a task that would contradict her claim that there is no need to examine the right to privacy any further.

I have suggested that mere ownership of possessions or the person does not adequately explain all privacy rights because there are cases in which privacy rights with respect to objects in the external world and the self do not correspond with their ownership. Though this strikes me as a severe, perhaps ultimately fatal, criticism of the reductionist program, Thomson is not incapable of responding to it. She might argue that the cases in which privacy rights do not correspond with property rights and rights over the person are mere flukes, which we might reasonably expect from such a fuzzy concept as privacy. Rather than dispute this contention, let us assume for the moment that it is correct—the majority of privacy rights correspond with property rights and rights over the person. Does this remove all problems from the course of Thomson's argument?

Thomson has to establish not merely that privacy rights correspond with property rights and rights over the person, but also that the character of this correspondence is a hierarchal one, that is, privacy rights are derived from other rights. To support her contention that privacy rights hold a secondary, derivative position, she argues that an appeal to "privacy" does not explain any of the rights of the privacy cluster: "I don't have a right to not be looked at because I have a right to privacy; I don't have a right that no one shall torture me in order to get personal information about me because I have a right to privacy; . . . it is because I have *these* rights that I have a right to privacy.[16] But I suggest that this argument is wrong. We have no reason to see ownership claims concerning material possessions and the body as necessarily more "primitive" than privacy claims. In fact, it is even plausible to suggest that *privacy* rights are more "basic" than other rights, especially property rights. For example, a Marxist might contend that the protection privacy extends over an individual's person naturally finds its expression in terms of property rights only in a capitalist society, which focuses on bodily property claims to the exclusion of the more basic category of privacy claims with respect to the person; for the Marxist, we should appeal to *privacy* rights to explain property rights. Since this example shows that privacy claims are not logically secondary to property claims, there is no clear reason to dismiss privacy claims in favor of property claims.

Assuming that Thomson could establish the priority of ownership-type rights over privacy rights, there remains a third and final hurdle for her argument. Even if we assume that all privacy claims *can* be derived from property rights and rights over the person, Thomson still has to establish that this fact entails her conclusion that we *should* abandon all discussion concerning the rights clustered under privacy on the grounds that it does nothing except add to our conceptual muddle. Although this entailment is crucial if the reductionist argument is to have any real force, Thomson slides over it rapidly: "if, as I take it, every right in the right to privacy cluster is also in some other right cluster, there is no need to find the that-which-is-in-common to all rights in the right to privacy cluster and no need to settle disputes about its boundaries."[17]

This claim that derivative status of privacy is in itself sufficient grounds to abandon discussion of privacy is fundamentally flawed. If we jump from the assumption that privacy rights are derivative to the conclusion that there is no need to discuss privacy, we neglect the fact that a cluster of derived claims can have a conceptual and normative significance irreducible to the meaning and value of the source from which it was derived. For example, consider the relation between the set of integers and the subset of primes. While it is true that every prime is an integer and that primes are a subset of integers, primes still possess a distinct nature and value for mathematics when compared to the set of integers. The possibility that this relation obtains in the case of privacy is not merely a logical possibility. The very fact that certain property and self-ownership rights can be divided off and placed in the privacy cluster suggests that there is a common factor shared by these apparently diverse rights. Otherwise, we are faced with the puzzling possibility that these absolutely unrelated rights have been grouped together arbitrarily.

Thomson might object at this point that the bare fact that we distinguish a privacy cluster of rights from other rights indicates nothing other than our confusion about privacy. This criticism contains a kernel of truth—it *is* possible that this distinction is arbitrary. But consider some of the results we reach if we assume that privacy rights are *nothing* other than ownership rights, lacking in both a distinct meaning and value. If this were the case, the meaning of any of my privacy claims would amount to, "That's mine, so others cannot access it." As for the wrong involved in violating these privacy claims, it would amount to the wrong of violating ownership claims; hence, all claims about the value of privacy amount to, "That's mine, so it's wrong of others to access it." Yet these results do not accord with our intuitions about privacy claims. When I state that my diary, personal conversations, home, parts of my body, and so forth, are protected by privacy, I *may* mean that I own them, but this does not exhaust my meaning. If it did, I could make privacy claims with reference to any of my possessions. However, as I have argued, this is not the case. I also mean that these are certain *sorts* of things, let us call them intimate things. Similarly, when I state that it is wrong to violate the privacy of my diary, personal conversations, home, parts of my body, and so forth, an element of this wrong *may* be attributable to the ownership violation, but this does not exhaust it. It is wrong to access these things not merely because they are mine, but more importantly because of the type of things they are—intimate things. For example, it may be wrong to access my diary simply because it is mine, but this element of wrong does not distinguish between the wrong of reading another's grocery list and her diary. It is wrong to read my diary not merely because it is mine, but also because of its intimacy. If someone were to ask me why it was wrong to read my diary, thereby violating my privacy, I would not merely exclaim, "It's mine!" Rather, I would indicate the nature of the thing being read,

"Look at what you're reading—it's personal!" If we accept that statements about the meaning and value of privacy rights contain intimacy claims *as well as* ownership claims, we must also accept that privacy rights are not indistinguishable from ownership rights. This amounts to a rejection of Thomson's claim that there is no need to search for the "that-which-is-in-common" to rights in the privacy cluster.

Thomson fails to establish the three points essential for her argument. First of all, all privacy claims cannot be expressed in terms of property and self-ownership claims. Second of all, assuming that privacy claims and property claims were to always correspond, we have no reason to think that privacy claims are derivative from other rights, rather than the other way around. Finally, even if we assume that privacy claims are a subset of property claims and claims about the person, this does not entail that discussion about this subset should be abandoned, since it appears to have a distinct nature and value rooted in intimacy.

A critic might interject that I have not succeeded in undermining the reductionist program. All I have done is to establish three claims. First, privacy claims do not appear to be expressible in terms of other claims. Second, even assuming that privacy claims are all expressible in terms of other claims, it remains unclear whether privacy claims are a set from which other claims are derived, or a subset derived from those claims. Third, even if we assume that privacy claims are a subset, we still have no reason to think that this subset lacks conceptual or moral importance. But it remains possible that other claims might be found that would more readily capture the core of privacy than was the case with ownership rights; furthermore, these claims might be established to be necessarily prior to privacy claims, while the subset of privacy claims might be established to be empty of any distinct meaning or value. I confess that this criticism is true—I have not established that the reductionist program is impossible. This must await my positive account of privacy. The argument in this chapter has been less ambitious: the reductionist program fails to offer us any reason to abandon our initial intuition that the nature and value of privacy *qua* privacy can be captured.

I have shown that we should not rush to abandon the concept of privacy when faced with reductionist skepticism. However, if we are to retain privacy as a distinct concept, we cannot stop at this point. The skeptic can still challenge us to define privacy and explain its value since we have argued that this can be done. This challenge can be neither evaded nor readily satisfied. If we evade it, the skeptic is left free to argue that our evasion indicates that privacy is *not* a morally or conceptually distinct concept—after all, the proponents of privacy don't even know what it is or why it is valuable! If we refer the skeptic to the privacy literature in an attempt to quell her challenge, the disagreement found in the literature will merely support her skepticism. We must go beyond tacitly accepting that the nature of privacy can be explained. The following chapters define privacy and explain its value.

Notes

1. Judith Jarvis Thomson, "The Right to Privacy," *Philosophy and Public Affairs* 4 (1975): 295–314. As I have pointed out in Chapter 2, the various privacy skeptics advance similar arguments. My survey of the literature convinces me that I am not doing the skeptical position a disservice in considering only Thomson's widely recognized paper. Furthermore, let me note that my criticisms of Thomson are similar to those raised by Thomas Scanlon's "Thomson on Privacy," *Philosophy and Public Affairs* 4 (1975): 315–322; and Jeffrey Reiman's "Privacy, Intimacy and Personhood," *Philosophy and Public Affairs* 6 (1976): 26–44.

2. Although Thomson's avowed goal is to clarify the *right* to privacy, I see no reason why her arguments must be understood as applying to privacy *qua* a right, rather than privacy *qua* a human interest. In what follows, I assume her arguments apply to privacy as an interest or right. Similarly, although I often use Thomson's rights-based terminology in this chapter, this does not entail any assumptions about the status of privacy. To avoid the appearance of any presumption, I intersperse my discussion of "privacy rights" with a discussion of "privacy interests" and "privacy claims"—these terms should be understood as synonyms.

3. Even if Thomson is justified in avoiding defining privacy, her argument that the *right* to privacy lacks coherence fails to entail that privacy itself cannot be defined; we can clearly define privacy in terms of the disparate rights it covers, even if such a definition runs the risk of triviality.

4. See, for example, Thomson, "The Right to Privacy," 303, 305.

5. Here "our bodies" should be understood in the broadest possible sense. It includes not only our physical bodies, but also such aspects of ourselves as our voices.

6. Thomson, "The Right to Privacy," 299.

7. Thomson, "The Right to Privacy," 305.

8. Thomson, "The Right to Privacy," 303.

9. Thomson, "The Right to Privacy," 305.

10. Thomson, "The Right to Privacy," 313.

11. Note that the violation in this case is not necessarily tied to the letters having a damaging content; my privacy would be violated even if the content of the love letters were innocuous, perhaps only innocent descriptions of my everyday life.

12. Thomson could reply to this example by claiming that ownership rights over the letters are not relinquished when I send them to another and, hence, privacy rights still exist. However, this would unduly expand the notion of property rights. Additionally, Thomson would then have to explain why certain letters (such as business letters) seem to possess no inherent property or privacy rights once they are sent. Even if Thomson were to argue that we are simply more prone to waive our property rights in the case of business letters than in the case of love letters, she would still be left with the task of explaining the special emphasis we place on access to love letters and why this emphasis is best described as primarily a property right and only secondarily as a privacy right.

13. This is not to suggest that nonintimate possessions *cannot* be the object of privacy claims—clearly they can, but not simply by virtue of being *possessions*.

14. Thomson could argue that we simply waive our privacy claims with respect to certain possessions, such as pens, yet retain them in the case of possessions such as diaries. This move falls victim to the criticisms I raised in note 12.

15. Thomson might reply to this criticism by arguing that these two cases are, at most, instances of my privacy being threatened, not actually violated—spying is merely an *attempt* to violate another's privacy. It is not until the spy actually *sees* (or senses) her intended victim that the victim's privacy is *violated*. The question is, does this distinction between privacy threats and privacy violations hold up under scrutiny? Is my privacy violated when the stranger on the bus manages to hear one word from my total conversation, but only threatened when she unsuccessfully attempts to listen (though still disturbing the course of the conversation)? Similarly, is my privacy only threatened if I remain completely removed from sight under my bed on the train all day, but violated when the edge of my hand is seen momentarily? In cases such as these, making a distinction between a threatened violation of privacy when an agent's voice or image has not been "stolen" and the "true" violation seems arbitrary at best.

16. Thomson, "The Right to Privacy," 312.

17. Thomson, "The Right to Privacy," 313.

4

Beyond Isolation: A Control-Based Account of Privacy

It is often argued that privacy is antithetical to publicity, that it works by separating the individual from others, restricting the access others have to particular areas of her life. While this separation-based account of the function of privacy may initially appear inescapable, there is an alternative: privacy may function by providing the individual with control over certain aspects of her life.[1] In what follows, I discuss these differing explanations of the function of privacy as embodied in both the philosophical literature and privacy law.[2] I contend that the differences fundamentally affect the domain of justified privacy claims and the value of privacy as a moral claim. Faced with this rift between separation-based and control-based definitions of privacy, I show that separation-based definitions deform the nature and value of privacy, while control-based definitions successfully capture the nature and value of privacy. Thus, this chapter explains the function of privacy in such a way as to overturn the apparent opposition between privacy and publicity.

The commonly accepted dichotomy between privacy and publicity is exemplified by Judith Jarvis Thomson's "The Right to Privacy" and by the field of tort privacy law.[3] Both definitions uphold the idea that privacy functions by keeping certain aspects of an individual's life or body strictly out of the public realm. According to Thomson, someone experiences privacy when she is neither looked at nor listened to, while she experiences privacy according to tort law when her "personal" matters are not exposed to the senses of others.[4] Despite their different accounts of content, Thomson and tort law agree on function—someone experiences privacy only to the degree she is left alone or separated from

41

the senses of others. This approach assumes that any exposure of a person's self to a "public" (even if this "public" is a group of intimates) necessarily detracts from her privacy. Before discussing the validity of this assumption, let us examine the alternative: control-based definitions of privacy.

Although separation-based definitions are prevalent in both the legal and philosophical literature, a different account of privacy's function appears in Thomas Scanlon's "Thomson on Privacy," James Rachels's "Why Privacy Is Important," and constitutional privacy law.[5] These discussions focus on the question of whether the individual is able to control the exposure of others to certain aspects of her life. Personal privacy is understood to be a measure of the control individuals have over the public's exposure to and regulation of these aspects of their lives. In particular, Scanlon suggests that the individual experiences privacy when she has control over a zone in which she can be free from certain types of intrusion.[6] For Rachels, privacy consists of the individual's control over access to and information about herself.[7] Finally, the definition used in constitutional privacy law accords the individual control over certain types of intimate decisions.[8] These control-based definitions are based on the shared assumption that privacy works in a significantly different way than it does according to Thomson and tort privacy law. Privacy is defined as a variety of freedom, a freedom that functions by granting the individual control over the division between the public and the private with respect to certain aspects of her life. Since an agent can exercise control by choosing to expose private aspects of her life to others, there is no necessary antagonism between privacy and publicity.

The difference between these views is not superficial; whether privacy is a state of control or simply separation from the public sphere fundamentally affects both our claims to be experiencing privacy and the value we place on it. To illustrate this, let us consider the domain and value of privacy according to both definitions with respect to a case involving a person locked in a bedroom. On the one hand, assume as correct Thomson's separation-based definition, privacy is not being looked at or listened to. Given this definition, a person locked in a bedroom who happens neither to be looked at nor listened to experiences privacy. As far as the value of her privacy is concerned, presumably she would claim that her "privacy" had a negative value. Her desire would be to lose privacy, rather than gain it. Now assume as correct a control-based definition. The person imprisoned in the bedroom no longer experiences privacy because she lacks control over who looks at her: any curious external party can decide to suddenly peer into her room. As far as the value of privacy is concerned, the agent would presumably describe her situation as characterized by an undesirable lack of privacy; privacy becomes a valuable, sought-after condition. The argument behind these examples is clear: we cannot avoid deciding between control-based and separation-based descriptions because they neither identify the same experiences as experiences of privacy nor delineate the same sphere of values.

Faced with the task of choosing between the two accounts, let us focus on separation-based definitions for the present, in particular, their appeal. To aid in this, I introduce a claim that I assume without argument constitutes a paradigmatic privacy claim: "I experience privacy in my home" (said by a woman who lives in an apartment with a friend). The appeal of separation-based definitions is that they accord with our tendency to think about privacy in terms of withdrawal from others rather than exposure to them—our speaker finds privacy in her home, not on the crowded street. Even when we think about the privacy in nonspatial contexts, we still place an emphasis on separation from the public realm, for example, we tend to describe the privacy of the family in terms of its separation from the power of the state and that of the body in terms of its separation from the access of others. This tendency to oppose privacy to publicity is not irrational; many paradigmatic experiences of privacy, such as the privacy our speaker finds in her home, *do* involve some degree of limited access to a person. Given that privacy and limited access or seclusion are, in fact, often conjoined, we can understand the temptation to claim that they are synonymous, leading to the separation-based privacy definitions.

Despite this, I suggest that we must reject separation-based definitions of privacy. That privacy often *manifests* itself in conjunction with limited access or separation does not mean that privacy *is* them. Although it is true that the person who states, "I experience privacy in my home," might correctly believe that some form of separation from others is essential to her privacy, it does not necessarily follow that this separation *is* her privacy. Let us consider some of the conclusions reached if we assume that privacy works through separation. First, privacy is neither necessarily desirable, nor necessarily undesirable, since separation is a neutral concept until it is placed within a particular context. Losing or gaining privacy carries no inherent moral connotation. Second, privacy is necessarily individualistic. As soon as one individual encounters another, no matter the nature of the encounter, privacy is necessarily lost. Third, many apparent "violations of privacy" are only threatened violations. As long as an individual remains separated from others, the strongest claim she can make is that her privacy is threatened. Establishing that any of these results are in conflict with the actual nature and value of privacy would undermine the assumption that privacy functions through separation. Let us consider whether this can be accomplished.

The first conclusion that stems from assuming privacy functions through separation is that privacy is inherently a morally neutral concept, one that gains a particular normative value only from its context. It develops because of the neutrality of the concept of separation; an agent can experience either the desirable separation of solitude or the undesirable separation of isolation, for example. But is privacy a value-free concept? Both our privacy intuitions and linguistic usage supports the "valued" nature of privacy. Our ordinary language reflects a predisposition toward treating privacy as a positively valued condition; for example, the response that comes to mind when someone announces that they have lost privacy is to commiserate with them, rather than to offer congratulations. Furthermore, we use the phrases "enjoying privacy" and "invasion of privacy" with their overt suggestions that privacy is valuable. Next, those cases that separation-based theories pass off as "undesirable privacy," such as the person who is separated from the senses of others because she is in a dungeon or trapped on an isolated island, are not easy to mesh with our privacy intuitions. We can imagine a shipwrecked person running to her rescuer and offering thanks for the relief of her isolation, but it is awkward at best to imagine this person praising her rescuer for relieving her privacy. Finally, a number of words describe conditions in which the individual and her activities are forcibly separated from the access of others, for example, censorship, isolation, deprivation, but these words could seldom be replaced with "privacy" and retain the appropriate undesirable value connotation; in fact, this is obviously false in most cases.

According to Anita Allen, my claim about the positive normative value of privacy can be refuted by pointing to any case in which privacy has been used for morally undesirable ends:

> I . . . maintain that privacy is neither a presumptive moral good nor a presumptive moral evil. Thus, one's enjoyment of the privacy of a cabin in the woods may merit moral approval as part of a plan to recover from a

nervous breakdown, but disapproval as part of a plan to neglect a dying spouse, abandoned and alone at home.[9]

Since we can readily find cases in which privacy seems to protect morally questionable or even reprehensible action, the privacy in these cases is itself morally tainted.

Allen's criticism conflates the value of privacy with the value of actions performed under its protection, however, the fact that a state is positively valued does *not* entail that all actions that embody it must share this value. For example, both liberty and free speech are commonly claimed to be positively valued states (within the context of liberalism), yet this clearly does not imply that every action that can be called an expression of liberty or every statement made as free speech shares this positive value. Saying that privacy, liberty, or free speech are positively valued states is equivalent to claiming that the burden of proof is upon the person who wishes to curtail privacy, liberty, or free speech—that person must offer a justification of her actions. This is not the case with a negatively valued concept such as "isolation": no justification is required for rescuing someone from isolation. Allen's argument fails to dislodge my argument that privacy possesses an inherently positive value. Furthermore, given the points I have made about privacy and language, we have no reason to accept that privacy is a neutral concept, which provides us with a reason to reject separation-based accounts of privacy's function.

Another problem developing from the assumption that privacy functions through separation is that it portrays privacy as essentially individualistic. If we assume that privacy consists of the agent having certain aspects of her life separated from others, then only the individual who is fully separated from others with respect to these aspects of her life will have full privacy. While I do not dispute the claim that the initial foundation of privacy is the individual, rather than the group, I question the claim that any grouping of individuals necessarily lessens the privacy of all concerned. This claim is faulty for two reasons: it gives the loss of privacy such a broad range as to make privacy a vacuous concept, and it makes it impossible to experience shared privacy.

To expand on my first point, if we assume that privacy is separation from some type of access from others, then it seems that the typical individual will constantly be experiencing privacy losses. For example, if we accept Thomson's definition of privacy as not being looked at or listened to, then we must also accept that the individual is constantly besieged with privacy invasions (unless we assume that she is constantly waiving her privacy claims—an obviously unlikely assumption). This seems to be simply false.

Turning to my second point, the individualism underlying separation-based privacy definitions appears to make shared privacy impossible. These accounts suggest that privacy has decreased in a wide range of cases that are not commonly considered in those terms; accordingly, I lose privacy when I willingly invite a close friend into my home, when I initiate mutual sexual activity with another, and when I allow a trusted friend to read a personal letter. The claim that these situations involve a privacy loss is opposed by both our linguistic and moral intuitions about privacy. Consider telling the other people involved in these examples, "I appreciate your lessening of my privacy." If we made this claim, others might question our understanding of the meaning of "privacy." Our impulse in these cases is to say that we are including another within our realm of privacy, not lessening our privacy (even in a desirable fashion). This linguistic intuition stems from an underlying intuition about the value of privacy; assuming that lost privacy is inherently undesirable, and that lessening our separation from others is not necessarily undesirable, it follows that lessening our separation from others is not always a loss of privacy, as suggested by separation-based accounts of privacy. In other words, publicity is not necessarily opposed to privacy. These arguments provide yet another reason to reject the claim that privacy functions through separation since separation-based accounts of privacy are unable to explain the relation between privacy and the individual.

The third argument against separation-based accounts of privacy is that they create a large class of "threatened privacy violations" that are more accurately described as true privacy violations. To illustrate this, consider two examples: (1) I realize that a peeping Tom is coming to my window, so I evade him by ducking under the bed; (2) a home dweller realizes that someone is attempting to overhear her conversation (but has not done so), so she drags her friend into the closet to continue the conversation. According to the separation-based definitions, these cases involve only a threatened privacy loss because the intruder never actually violates the agent's physical or verbal separation. I suggest that this is incorrect.

Let us assume that either the peeping Tom manages to catch sight of my foot or the covert listener manages to hear one word of conversation.

The separation-based definitions of privacy would claim that these trivial additions transform the situations into actual privacy violations. But I see no reasonable distinction between these cases and the original cases with their burdensome protective maneuvers. Rather, the core of the privacy violation seems to lie in the need to attempt concealment in a zone that is intended to be under the agent's control. We can see the thinness of the wedge that the separation-based definitions attempt to drive between these cases when we consider whether I in my position under the bed or the person conversing in the closet would claim a merely threatened privacy violation; clearly both of us would claim a very real one. It seems slightly ridiculous to imagine either myself under the bed or the woman in the closet calling out to the invader, ''You are threatening my privacy,'' rather than, ''You are invading my privacy''—the former claim would lead others to doubt that either of us understood the meaning of ''privacy.'' As separation-based definitions do not allow for our intuition that privacy can be damaged, not merely threatened, when someone is still separated from the access of others, they suffer from yet another shortcoming.

Now that I have presented my arguments against separation-based definitions of privacy, criticizing these definitions for their value neutrality, inability to explain shared privacy, and failure to account for privacy violations in cases where access has not actually been breached, my conclusion is obvious: separation-based definitions of privacy fail. But, accepting my argument, we are faced with the question of whether control-based definitions of privacy are more satisfactory. I believe that they are.

Upon consideration, it may first appear that claiming privacy works through the mechanism of control does not reflect the positive value of privacy to any greater degree than separation-based theories. The concept of ''control'' seems to share the value-neutrality I criticized in the concept of ''separation,'' for example, ''mind control'' does not invoke anything inherently positive. But let us consider how control works within the framework provided by privacy. As I have previously pointed out, control-based definitions of privacy function by giving the *individual* control over a certain area of *her own* life, in other words, they give the individual a specified realm of autonomy. Given the modern liberal assumption that autonomy is a positively valued condition, we are led to the conclusion that control-based definitions of privacy do incorporate an underlying assumption that privacy is positively valued. Of course, that positive value does not trump the value of all other rights and interests; it does not entail that an agent's control over the private domain can never be justifiably curtailed. It does entail that any curtailment of the individual's control over the domain of the private must be justified; in such a case, the justification must be sufficiently strong to overcome the positive value liberalism places on autonomy.

The second problem faced by separation-based accounts of privacy was their inability to explain shared privacy except in terms of lessened privacy for the individuals involved. Control-based definitions of privacy offer a more plausible explanation. If we assume that privacy can be defined as the individual having control over a certain area of her life, then we are not forced to say, for example, that asking intimates into our home involves a loss of privacy. A control-based account of privacy, such as Rachels's definition of privacy as having control over access to and information about oneself, makes the invitation to these intimates consistent with a claim of undamaged privacy: by inviting them in, we are merely exercising the control that privacy grants.

The objection might be raised that the assumption that privacy is a state of control makes privacy definitions too inclusive in describing cases of shared privacy. For example, let us imagine a situation in which I voluntarily open my door and allow a salesperson to enter my house. Upon entry, she starts to read my correspondence on the table and refuses to refrain from this activity. According to the criticism I am considering, this situation with its obvious privacy violation would be described by control-based privacy theorists as "shared privacy." I exercised control in permitting the salesperson to come in; thus, if control is the core of privacy, my privacy has not been violated.

This objection fails because of its overly simplistic notion of control. Someone does not necessarily control a situation simply by virtue of having initiated it; for example, the mere fact that I control the physical movements involved in getting into a car and driving it down the street does not entail that I control the situation when the car's brakes suddenly fail, leaving me careening down the street. Similarly, the fact that I may momentarily control an aspect of a situation does not mean that I control the situation; in the above example, if I gain control of my car for a moment, I am not in control of the situation as a whole. Exercising control is an ongoing process; as such, it consists of not only the voluntary initiation of a situation, but also the ability to regulate the situation as it develops (which includes the ability to either continue or halt it) and a reasonable expectation of continued control. Furthermore, an agent must be able to exercise this regulative ability with respect to her desired end, rather than an arbitrary or imposed end; if I find that I can regulate my car's behavior when it comes to spinning in circles, but my desired end is driving down the road, I am not in control of the car in that particular situation. Given this explanation of control, the situations that involved asking friends into the home and asking in the privacy-violating salesperson are not identical as far as control is concerned. In the case of the friends, I have not only initiated the situation, I also control their continued presence, and I have the reasonable expectation that I could successfully ask them to leave, an expectation that is backed up by a complex web of social conventions and norms of friendship.[10] There are no barriers to prevent me from using this regulative ability according to the dictates of my desired ends. In the case of the salesperson, I have initiated the situation of her entry, but my control over the situation stopped at that point. The first situation is one of shared privacy; the second one is not. Thus, the criteria for shared privacy set up by control-based definitions of privacy do not create an unlimited domain of shared privacy since few situations offer the agent all the conditions necessary for the true exercise of control.

There is a third problem: are control-based definitions of privacy capable of explaining how privacy can be violated when access to a person is only seriously threatened? I believe they are. Let us consider the previously discussed case of the person who had to crawl under a bed to evade the gaze of a peeping Tom. Focusing on the question of whether the person under the bed is in control of the situation, it seems that the answer is obvious: she is not; therefore, she is experiencing a privacy violation if we assume privacy functions through control. Of course, a critic might contend that she actually *is* in control of the situation—after all, *she* crawled under the bed. This argument falls victim to my previous discussion of the conditions necessary for control, according to which crawling under the bed does not entail that the crawler is in control of the situation; she also has to possess the freedom to crawl out without being accessed (if that is her desired end) and a reasonable expectation of dictating access to herself in the immediate future.

My argument that control-based privacy explains why certain cases of seriously threatened access are true privacy violations is open to the criticism that it sweeps too broadly, destroying any distinction what-soever between actual and threatened privacy violations by transforming all threatened violations into actual violations. The immediate response to this criticism is evident: assuming that privacy is control-based does not mean abandoning the distinction between actual and threatened violations. Privacy is violated when an agent loses control over the private realm, while it is merely threatened when her control over the private realm is attacked but remains intact. Unfortunately this response is not sufficient to quiet the above criticism. The core of the criticism is that the notion of control is insufficient to drive a wedge between threatened and actual privacy violations; control-based definitions of privacy *necessarily* conflate the two. To illustrate, let us consider several variations on the peeping Tom scenario. In the first version, a peeping Tom looks in a window and sees a person. In the second version, the peeping Tom looks in a window, but does not see the intended object because she has concealed herself under the bed to avoid his gaze. In the third version, a person learns that a peeping Tom has been seen in her small neighborhood. Examining these, our immediate intuition is that they are not all privacy violations. While the first two seem clear violations, the last seems to represent only a privacy threat. The line of criticism I am considering claims that this basic intuition cannot be accommodated by control-based accounts of privacy. The problem is that we can describe the person in each example as losing control due to the peeping Tom: The person in the first version lost control of access to herself because she was seen; the person in the second version lost control because she had to dive under the bed to avoid the peeping Tom; the person in the last example lost control because there exists a reasonable chance that the peeping Tom could try to gain visual access to her without her permission. Given that we can describe each person as having lost control, aren't we forced to call them all privacy violations?

This criticism assumes that a person has lost control whenever she lacks the ability to perfectly regulate future events with respect to her desired end. According to this, even the mere fact that a peeping Tom exists causes me to lose control (and, hence, privacy) because I cannot control the remote possibility that this person might try to look at me, forcing me to take evasive action or be seen. Though this is a possible interpretation of what it means to have control, it is not a very plausible one. It entails that we could never truthfully claim, "I control *X*," because of the inescapable indeterminacy of the future. There is a more plausible interpretation: our control over a situation is threatened, but not violated, when we are faced with a high probability that the situation will involve factors we have not personally determined. These factors have to be such that they could reasonably be expected to exert sufficient causal influence over our particular ends in the given situation as to require protective action to gain that end. We have control in situation X when there exists a reasonable probability that we could regulate the outcome of the situation without recourse to emergency maneuvers.[11] This explanation of control not only makes it correct for us to claim, "I control X," despite an inability to predict future events, but also explains why control-based definitions of privacy do not conflate privacy threats and violations—privacy is threatened only when a reasonable person has to take protective measures to restrict access to her private domain, but violated when either these measures are required to be emergency measures or access is actually gained.[12] Hence, in the peeping Tom examples, the first two are true privacy violations; when the person is either seen or has to hide under a bed (clearly an emergency measure), she is forced to take protective measures to prevent the access (or further access) of the peeping Tom to her private domain. The final example, on the other hand, with its scenario of a person learning that a peeping Tom is in her neighborhood, presents only a privacy threat. Thus, defining privacy in terms of control accounts for privacy violations that do not involve actual access, while refraining from transforming all situations involving a threat into violations.

Having established that by assuming privacy functions through control, we can account for the problems that beset separation-based accounts of privacy—explaining the positive value of privacy, the existence of "shared privacy," and the existence of privacy violations that do not involve access—this assumption seems to be established on a firm foundation. But the ability of this assumption to respond to the problems surrounding the assumption based on separation does not prove its validity beyond a question. There remains a final problem: is this explanatory power provided at the cost of flaws within the assumption itself, problems that did not develop in the case of separation-based theories? Many theorists who support separation-based definitions argue that this is indeed the case.[13] The flaw they find hidden in control-based definitions is that they make it impossible to relinquish privacy, as Ruth Gavison argues:

> "control" suggests that the important aspect of privacy is the ability to choose it and see that the choice is respected. All possible choices are

consistent with enjoyment of control, however, so that defining privacy in terms of control relates it to the power to make certain choices rather than to the way in which we exercise this power. But individuals may choose to have privacy or to give it up.[14] . . . an individual may voluntarily choose to disclose everything about himself to the public. This disclosure obviously leads to a loss of privacy despite the fact that it involved an exercise of control.[15]

Gavison and other critics of the assumption that privacy functions through control contend that this assumption makes it impossible to escape from within privacy because every choice is an exercise of control.

Let us consider the core of the above criticism: " 'control' suggests that the important aspect of privacy is the ability to choose it and see that the choice is respected. All possible choices are consistent with enjoyment of control."[16] At first glance, this claim seems true: if I freely make a choice, I am in control of my choice. But, as I have discussed, being in control of a situation requires far more than simply initiating the situation or controlling any particular slice of the situation as a whole. It also requires both being able to regulate or even halt the progression of the situation with respect to a desired end and possessing a reasonable certainty that this ability will be retained in the future.[17] Given this account of control, it is not difficult to develop examples in which people give up their privacy. Consider Gavison's case of a person who discloses everything about herself to the public, thereby losing privacy. Gavison claims the person exercises control in doing this; this claim is incorrect given my explanation of control. If I give information to strangers, I loss control of it since I can no longer regulate its future dissemination.[18] Thus, the person in Gavison's example has relinquished control over the revealed information, despite the fact that he controlled the initiation of this process of revelation; he cannot halt or regulate the process he has started, no matter his future wishes. He has put aside privacy. As this examples shows, assuming privacy functions through control does not mean that privacy cannot be forgone; we can choose to lose control of privacy-protected information, access, and actions. The fact that we make the initial choice to lose control does not entail that the attendant situation is also under our control.

Setting aside this web of claim, criticism, and countercriticism, my conclusion is obvious: privacy functions through control. Control-based definitions of privacy, such as those offered by Scanlon, Rachels, and constitutional privacy law, explain our intuitions about how privacy works much more satisfactorily than do separation-based definitions, such as those presented by Thomson and tort privacy law. We have every reason to embrace the idea that privacy provides people with control over some area or areas of their lives, even though this assumption overthrows the commonly accepted antithesis between privacy and publicity. Obviously, this leads to a new question: if privacy functions by granting the individual control over X, what is X? The next chapter responds to this problem.

Notes

1. I have separated the question of how privacy functions from the question of privacy's content, so this chapter does not describe the "particular areas of . . . life" covered by privacy. This is not to suggest that identifying the content of privacy is unimportant—it is important, and I take it up in the next chapter. Despite this fact, the argument here occasionally requires that I assume something about content, and at these points, I will *provisionally* assume that privacy's content covers informational access, physical access, and certain of the agent's decisions about her own actions. Hence, when I talk about an agent having privacy with respect to a domain of life, the content of that domain might include matters of access or matters of liberty with respect to decisions. I will set aside until another chapter the question of whether being in control over what we do is related to being in control over information about ourselves.

2. A critic might interject at this point that I am not truly working with two distinct accounts of the function of privacy. After all, control and separation are clearly not antithetical categories; privacy might be a state of separation from others that provides the agent with control. However, the control-based accounts of privacy are not exclusively concerned with control through separation; some are concerned with providing the agent control over her actions, whether or not this control is gained through separation. This is particularly apparent in constitutional privacy law. As David A. J. Richards notes, "it [constitutional privacy] involves affirmative personal rights . . . . In *Roe*, the challenged law subjected the person performing the abortion to criminal sanctions and was unconstitutional because it made it difficult for women to obtain the desired service"; see David A. J. Richards, "The Jurisprudence of Privacy as a Constitutional Right," in *Privacy*, ed. William Bier (New York: Fordham University Press, 1980), 139. Hence, I believe my distinction between separation and control-based accounts of privacy is necessary to do justice to the literature.

3. Judith Jarvis Thomson, "The Right to Privacy," *Philosophy and Public Affairs* 4 (1975): 295–314; tort privacy law is discussed in countless legal articles, but a useful survey of important tort privacy cases is to be found in P. Allan Dionisopoulos and Craig Ducat, *The Right to Privacy* (St. Paul: West Publishing Co., 1976). I am using Thomson's privacy definition and that found in tort privacy law only to illustrate the use of separation-based privacy definitions—they do not exhaust the category.

4. Thomson, "The Right to Privacy," 300; Dionisopoulos and Ducat, *The Right to Privacy,* 19.

5. Thomas Scanlon, "Thomson on Privacy," *Philosophy and Public Affairs* 4 (1975): 315–22; James Rachels, "Why Privacy Is Important," *Philosophy and Public Affairs* 4 (1975): 323–33. As was the case with tort privacy, accounts of constitutional privacy law can be found in countless legal articles. A good place to start is David A. J. Richards, *Toleration and the Constitution* (New York: Oxford University Press, 1986).

6. See Scanlon, "Thomson on Privacy," especially p. 320. Although Scanlon is not explicit in saying that privacy must function through control, I believe this claim can be extracted from his paper.

7. Rachels, "Why Privacy Is Important," 326.

8. See, for example, Griswold v. Connecticut, 381 U.S. 479 (1965); Eisenstadt v. Baird, 405 U.S. 438 (1972); and Stanley v. Georgia, 394 U.S. 557 (1969).

9. Anita Allen, *Uneasy Access: Privacy for Women in a Free Society* (Rowman and Littlefield, 1988), 18.

10. It is important to note that we can have control over a situation involving our friends without actually possessing physical power over them—the social conventions of friendship ensure such control. This reveals that control is usually a product of social conventions that acknowledge and protect individual agency, rather than a product of raw physical power. Of course, this is not to deny that social conventions, such as laws, are often upheld by physical power.

11. To illustrate these points, imagine a situation in which a person is riding her bike on a path toward a tack (a path from which she cannot escape), which will if hit puncture the bike's tire and cause an accident. There are several outcomes open to the bike rider: (a) she can hit the tack and crash; (b) she can see the tack immediately before striking it and crash her bike to avoid the tack; (c) she can see the tack a reasonable length of time before hitting it and come to a stop to avoid it. According to my explanation of control, the bike rider has lost control of the situation in both (a) and (b), while (c) involves a situation of a merely threatened loss of control. Thus, when the bike rider has to take protective measures (stopping her bike), measures that she would not take otherwise, her control is threatened. The closer the bike rider comes to being forced to perform emergency maneuvers, the greater is the threat presented to her control. If she is actually

forced to perform such maneuvers, she has lost control, even though she might conceivably regain it through her actions.

12. Clearly a line-drawing problem emerges at this point concerning how to distinguish between protective and emergency measures. We might distinguish between them on the grounds that protective measures are characterized by some degree of choice on the agent's part, while emergency measures are not. I make no claims that this is either a sharp or readily discovered division.

13. See, for example, Anita Allen, *Uneasy Access.* Also, see Ruth Gavison, "Privacy and the Limits of Law," in *Philosophical Dimensions of Privacy: An Anthology,* ed. Ferdinand Schoeman (New York: Cambridge University Press, 1984), 346–402; and William A. Parent, "Recent Work on the Concept of Privacy," *American Philosophical Quarterly* 20 (1983): 341–55.

14. Gavison, "Privacy and the Limits of Law," 350.

15. Gavison, "Privacy and the Limits of Law," 384, note 23.

16. Gavison, "Privacy and the Limits of Law," 350.

17. To illustrate this, imagine a person willingly getting into a car and deciding that her desired end was to race it through the mountains at high speeds; we would not claim that she was in control of the car-racing situation if she could not stop or her car were constantly plunging wildly off the road despite her desires.

18. The importance of restricting this information distribution to strangers is that the fact that I am informing *strangers* is relevant to my loss of control. If I tell information to friends, I forgo physical control of the information, but often still retain equally effective control due to social norms and the ties of friendship. Strangers do not possess duties to conceal information that has been revealed to them, hence control over information is unquestionably relinquished when it is conveyed to a stranger. This example illustrates that we can possess or lack control over a situation not only due to considerations that are intrinsic to the agent's capacities, but also due to extrinsic considerations such as social norms.

5

Information, Access, or Intimate Decisions about Our Actions? The Content of Privacy

An agent possesses privacy to the extent that she has control over certain aspects of her life. But which aspects? In other words, what is the content of privacy? Three potential lines of response to these questions emerge from the legal and philosophical literature. First of all, privacy might regulate information about ourselves[1]; second of all, privacy might concern access to ourselves[2]; and finally, privacy might focus on intimate decisions about our actions.[3] I term these responses, respectively, "information-based," "access-based," and "decision-based" accounts of privacy's content.[4] In what follows, I argue that the content of privacy cannot be captured if we focus exclusively on either information, access, or intimate decisions because privacy involves all three areas. Furthermore, I suggest that these apparently disparate areas are linked by the common denominator of intimacy—privacy's content covers *intimate* information, access, and decisions. I conclude by offering a definition of privacy that cuts across the standard categories of information, access, or intimate decisions: privacy is the state of the agent having control over a realm of intimacy, which contains her decisions about intimate access to herself (including intimate informational access) and her decisions about her own intimate actions.

Though there are three contenders for the content of privacy, one stands apart from the others due to its extensive use in everyday, legal, and philosophical discourse—privacy involves information about an agent.[5] This extensive usage is readily illustrated. In everyday life, when another learns a carefully concealed fact about our sex life, behavior at home, or personal habits, we are quick to label this dissemination of information as a privacy violation.[6] In such a case, we would explain that our privacy has been violated because it is wrong for others to distribute or obtain such personal information without our permission. Our everyday intuitions about the ties between privacy and information are mirrored in the domain of law and legislation, where privacy often assumes the role of protecting information about the individual; for example, tort privacy law is largely concerned with information protection,[7] and state privacy legislation is chiefly designed to guard certain types of information about the agent, including information about her credit, medical, and educational history.[8] Finally, privacy theorists put forward such a quantity of information-based privacy definitions that understanding privacy's content in terms of information has been termed a "dogma" of privacy theory.[9] In perhaps the most well-known privacy definition, Alan Westin explains that privacy is "the claim of individuals, groups, or institutions to determine for themselves when, how, and to what extent information about them is communicated to others."[10] Given this proliferation of appeals to information, clearly an adequate account of privacy's content must either explicitly include or exclude information. In what follows, I argue that some, but not all, information must be included within privacy's scope.

Many common claims concerning information constitute representative privacy claims. This is readily illustrated. Imagine that I claim my privacy has been violated when I learn another person has informed the world in great detail about my sexual proclivities, despite my explicit request to the contrary. Two points concerning my claim are clear. First, my protest is directed against the information dissemination that has taken place; if asked why I was protesting, I might explain that others should not know detailed information about my sexual activity without my permission. Second, my identification of this information claim as a privacy claim seems to be beyond dispute. If someone were to deny this, I would not leap to the conclusion that *my* definition of privacy was in error—I would question whether *they* understood the meaning of "privacy" and suggest that *their* definition of privacy was flawed. The argument underlying this example is simple—information cannot be altogether excluded from the content of privacy.

Assuming that privacy's content is partially informational, should we allow that privacy's content is exclusively informational, that privacy is nothing more than the state of possessing control over information about ourselves? Although I accept that personal information is a component of privacy's content, I do not accept it as the identifying and constraining feature. The first problem faced by an information-based definition is that the fact that something is a piece of information about an agent is not a sufficient condition for it being within the scope of privacy. In other words, privacy does not involve control over *all* information about ourselves.[11] To illustrate this, consider a variety of successful attempts to gain information about me. Imagine that a stranger wishes to find out information about my sexual proclivities. She learns the desired information from my excessively talkative friend.[12] Imagine that the stranger wishes to learn where I park my car. She learns this information from the same revealing friend.[13] Each of these cases involves an obvious loss of control over information; however, they are not both obvious cases of lost privacy. The first case seems to involve a loss of privacy; in fact, assuming that my friend culpably distributed information, she has violated my privacy. The second case seems not to involve a privacy loss. To support these intuitions, consider what would happen if I accused my friend of lessening my privacy in the first case: the burden of proof would be on my friend to explain why a privacy loss had not occurred. If she rejected this burden, I would simply point to the nature of the information she revealed, ''Look at what you revealed! It's intimate!'' Without extenuating circumstances, the intimacy of sexual information places it squarely within the parameters of privacy. Yet, if I made the same accusation in the second case, the burden of proof would remain with me—*despite* the fact that there has clearly been a loss of information about myself. I would still have to justify my inclusion of car-parking information within the scope of privacy. The impersonal, nonintimate nature of information about a parking place usually places it outside of privacy's reach.[14] As these examples reveal, neither the presence nor the absence of a privacy loss can be explained by citing the presence of absence of information distribution. We must look at the *type* of information disseminated; it is the *intimacy* of this information that identifies a loss of privacy.[15]

My argument is open to the criticism that I have drawn privacy's content closer to our linguistic intuitions only to abandon our moral intuitions: defining privacy in terms of intimate information, rather than information as a whole, fails to account for certain of our moral intuitions. The argument supporting this criticism consists of two steps. The first step points out that including intimate information within the content of privacy allows us to morally condemn another when she culpably damages our control over intimate information—she has violated our privacy. However, excluding nonintimate information from the content of privacy has the opposite effect: we cannot condemn another for culpably lessening our control over nonintimate information since the damage does not truly constitute a privacy loss due to the nature of the information involved. The second step is prescriptive: since it is factually true that damaging someone's control over nonintimate information about herself is often morally reprehensible, it is incorrect to limit privacy's protection to intimate information. It renders us unable to condemn morally reprehensible instances of lessening another's control over nonintimate information. In order to analyze this argument, two questions must be addressed. Does an agent ever possess a moral claim to control nonintimate information about herself? If so, is this protection best described in terms of privacy?

The answer to the first question is not open to significant debate. The moral culpability of lessening or destroying an individual's control over nonintimate information in certain circumstances is readily illustrated. Imagine that a talkative friend of mine asks me what I am doing tomorrow. I reply that I am giving a surprise party for a mutual friend. My talkative friend conveys this information to others, ruining the surprise. Similarly, imagine that I tell a friend that I have taken a new job. I warn her not to repeat this information, as I wish to tell people myself. Despite this warning, she does inform others, frustrating my desire to provide the news. Do each of these examples involve morally blameworthy damage to the agent's control over nonintimate information? Yes. First of all, each of these cases involves an obvious information loss. Second of all, the information lost in both cases is not intimate. According to our society's norms, general information about a person's party plans and employment is not sufficiently personal to merit the heading of "intimate."[16] If a casual acquaintance asked me about the date of a non-surprise party I was giving or the nature of my job, I might deny her this information for reasons of my own, but an exclamation of, "That's not something you should ask me about!" would be a puzzling and incomplete explanation of the reasons for my denial.[17] Finally, assuming a lack of mitigating factors, both of these examples involve morally blameworthy action on the part of the information spreader. The information-damaged individual can justifiably make a moral claim against the damager, on the grounds that the party or job information *ought* not to have been distributed without prior permission. These two examples demonstrate that my critic is at least partially correct. There are cases in which damaging someone's control over nonintimate information is morally culpable; hence, the agent does possess a moral claim to control nonintimate information about herself in certain circumstances. But is privacy a suitable foundation for this claim?

Given the chaos that surrounds privacy, it is not surprising that privacy appeals are often used to ground claims to control nonintimate information. For example, many laws and government regulations prohibiting the unauthorized distribution of nonintimate information about citizens are couched in terms of privacy.[18] However, I believe this common usage confuses privacy with secrecy. An appeal to secrecy serves as an appropriate descriptive and normative foundation for our claims to control nonintimate information about ourselves and our moral condemnation of those who damage this control. To illustrate this, reconsider my previous example of the talkative friend and the surprise party information. When I tell my friend about the planned party and add, "It's a secret," my added comment conveys two meanings to my friend—the descriptive implication that the party plans are concealed information and the normative implication that she ought not inform others about my plans. If my friend proceeds to tell others, spoiling my party plans, I can explain her moral culpability by pointing to the fact that she has unjustifiably destroyed my secrecy. As this example shows, secrecy can be used to accurately describe our regulation of nonintimate information and to capture the prescriptive significance of such regulation.

A question remains unanswered: why should we prefer "secrecy" to "privacy"? After all, privacy can be used as I described above.[19] Secrecy has several advantages over privacy when it comes to accurately describing control over nonintimate information. First, secrecy does not possess underlying suggestions of intimacy, as is the case with privacy. Hence, using secrecy to describe our control over nonintimate information allows us to preserve the link between privacy and intimacy. Second, secrecy is not an inherently positive concept, unlike privacy: we lack a fundamental right or claim to secrecy.[20] This accords with the fact that regulating nonintimate information about ourselves is not always morally acceptable—we have no right to control nonintimate information simply *qua* nonintimate information; to establish such a claim, we have to explain the plans that somehow justify this control. If a census taker asks me about the number of rooms in my house, I cannot usually justifiably respond, ''You have no business knowing that information!'' In contrast, the positive value accorded to privacy makes privacy claims valid largely independently of our plans; the foundation of such claims lies in the fact that intimate information is, indeed, *intimate* information. Third, distinguishing secrecy from privacy allows us to distinguish between what we fear from a loss of secrecy and a loss of privacy. Secrecy involves concealing information from a specific class of people, those who could potentially damage your interests if they knew the information. As Morton Levine notes, secrecy involves concealing ''information which one feels would render one vulnerable to some kind of damage. . . . If the limits of your assets were known to a potential landlord, he might not grant you a lease.''[21] The same type of concealment is also what is at stake in the case of nonintimate information regulation. For example, when I appeal to my friend not to tell others about my surprise party or new job, my goal is to conceal this information from specific others—if the people from whom I wished to conceal the information somehow learned about it, I would no longer be concerned about its concealment because I would no longer fear having my plans damaged. This contrasts with privacy, since our concern in privacy cases is to control information, not simply conceal it from those who might damage us with it. Control requires regulating information with respect to others whether or not they present any threat of damaging our interests; when I seek privacy with respect to my diary, I seek to control it with respect to humanity as a whole—I fear *anyone* accessing it without my permission. Given these points, it is clear that secrecy is capable of explaining why violating another's control over nonintimate information is morally questionable; it also provides a more satisfactory account than that provided by privacy. Hence, the conclusion is clear: privacy need not include nonintimate information within its scope if we are to explain morally reprehensible curtailments of nonintimate information control.[22]

At this point, I have modified the sufficient condition for something to be within the scope of privacy—it must not be merely information about an agent, but intimate information. However, even with this modification, information-based accounts of privacy's content still face a problem—an information loss, even a loss of intimate information, does not constitute a necessary condition for a privacy loss. It can be lost without another actually gaining information. There are two ways in which this can occur. First of all, a privacy loss can occur when the loss of information is only threatened. My previous example of a peeping Tom failing to see a person concealed under a bed illustrates how this might happen. In this case, the peeping Tom might be construed as having gained some form of access to the concealed individual, but clearly this has not taken the form of information acquisition. Yet the privacy loss nevertheless exists.[23] Second of all, privacy can be lost when access is breached without a gain of information. For example, when a peeping Tom looks in a person's window for the *second* time, it is conceivable that he might acquire absolutely no new information about the victim. Despite this failure, the peeping Tom clearly violates the victim's privacy with the second, as well as the first, inspection. When he is charged with the second violation, he cannot escape with the explanation, "I've seen it all before!"

An intimate information-based definition of privacy will necessarily be incomplete because the loss of privacy need not involve the loss of information; yet the tie between intimate information and privacy cannot be escaped. Faced with this need to preserve the link between intimate information and privacy, while denying that intimate information is the sole constituent of privacy, let us consider the privacy accounts that claim to accomplish this: access-based definitions.

Access-based privacy definitions come in a multitude of forms. For example, Thomas Scanlon suggests that privacy provides us with a zone within which we need not be on the alert against intrusions and observations.[24] James Rachels and Jeffrey Reiman contend that privacy provides us with control over who has access, including informational access, to us.[25] Despite such variations, access-based definitions share an assumption about the content of privacy: it covers access to the agent.[26] Hence, the generic model of a control-based, access-focused privacy definition amounts to the following: privacy is the state of an agent possessing control over access to herself. With this model in mind, let us consider two questions. Does defining privacy's content in terms of access avoid the difficulties that beset information-based definitions? Does access to an individual cover all aspects of privacy's content? I believe that access-based privacy definitions are only partially successful at capturing privacy's content.

I concluded my criticism of information-based accounts of privacy with a question: how can we include intimate information within the scope of privacy, while acknowledging that the dissemination of information is not necessary for the loss of privacy? Explaining privacy's content in terms of access to an individual enables us to explain how it can be lost both with *and* without the actual loss of information. On the one hand, if we accept that privacy is concerned with the regulation of access to an agent, then information loss is not necessary for the loss of privacy because an agent can damage another's access control without learning information about her; for example, a peeping Tom who looks at a victim for the tenth time is clearly damaging the victim's control over access to herself, even if no new information is revealed. On the other hand, a loss of control over intimate information can still be a privacy loss because an agent can access another by learning information about her. In other words, learning information about another can be understood as informational access, a subset of access.[27] To illustrate how a revelation of information might be an access violation, imagine that an individual manages to obtain another's love letters, which she reads without the owner's permission. This act of information acquisition is an access violation—the letter reader unjustifiably gains access to another through learning the information contained in the letters. In short, access-based definitions explain why the loss of control over information is a possible, but not necessary, route to a privacy loss—information is only one way to gain access to another.

However, access-based definitions of privacy are not without problems. The first one is familiar: access is not always a sufficient condition for a privacy loss. Not all forms of access diminish privacy. On the one hand, intimate access to another clearly lessens her privacy, for example, staring persistently at her, grabbing her breast, listening intently to her discussion with a friend, or learning about her sexual habits. On the other hand, nonintimate forms of access do not involve the loss of privacy. Consider the countless ways in which others access us in the course of an ordinary day: glancing at us, brushing against us in passing, hearing fragments of our conversations, learning pieces of information about our dress, hair color, and posture. Such casual, nonintimate forms of access differ in kind, rather than only in degree, from privacy-lessening forms of intimate access. To illustrate this, consider what would be a reasonable response to a person who protested her privacy was lessened by such forms of nonintimate access. We would point to the *type* of access involved, stressing the point that this *type* of access does not constitute a decrease of privacy. If she rejected this explanation, the burden of proof would be on *her* to convince us that these apparently nonintimate, nonprivate forms of access were, in reality, sufficiently intimate to merit privacy. If privacy claims concerning access have to be couched in terms of intimacy, then we must reject unmodified access definitions of privacy.[28]

We have found a sufficient condition for a loss of privacy in the form of violating another's control over intimate access to herself. However, although many privacy issues revolve around access regulation, that does not exhaust the field of privacy. Intimate decisions also appear to fall within the scope of privacy, as is evident in both law and our everyday intuitions; for example, questions of access are peripheral to the majority of constitutional privacy cases. Constitutional law focuses on "a privacy interest with reference to certain *decisions* that are properly for the individual to make."[29] The decisions that the Supreme Court has protected under the rubric of privacy include those about such intimate activities as child rearing and education, family relationships, procreation, marriage, contraception, and abortion.[30] The Court's rationale for including an agent's decisions about such activities within the content of privacy explicitly appeals to their *intimacy;* according to the Court, it is *because* such decisions are intimate that they belong within the sphere of an agent's constitutional right to privacy. This inclusion is not peculiar to the Supreme Court. We commonly distinguish between intimate and nonintimate decisions about our actions, characterizing intimate decisions as "private" or "personal"—unfit subjects for the state's regulatory power. Consider the difference between being informed that the social welfare mandates that we must engage in sexual activity with specified individuals and being informed that the social welfare mandates that we must pay taxes. Our liberty of action is curtailed in each case, yet these curtailments are not identical. Decisions concerning sexual activity and sexual partners are not the type of decisions that can be dictated by the social welfare, barring extraordinary social hardship, while the social welfare seems a reasonable justification for taxes. If asked to justify these different conclusions, we might respond that the decision to engage in sex with a particular individual is a private matter—our privacy is damaged if the decision is forced—while decisions about taxes are neither intimate nor private. This response constitutes an understandable defense. It accords with our underlying intuition that intimate decisions about our actions belong with the realm of privacy, while nonintimate decisions about our actions fall outside of this realm. Given this legal and everyday intuition that constitutional privacy issues are part of privacy's content, must we discard our definition of privacy in terms of the agent's control over intimate access?[31] Not necessarily.

Faced with the apparent conflict between decisional and access accounts of privacy, some have argued that "decisional privacy" is a misnomer: it is actually nothing more than liberty or freedom attached to a misleading description. As Ruth Gavison explains, "identifying privacy as noninterference with private action . . . may obscure the nature of the legal decision and draw attention away from important considerations. The limit of state interference with individual action is an important question that has been with us for centuries. The usual terminology for dealing with this question is that of 'liberty of action.'"[32] According to this view, claiming that intimate decisions are protected by privacy is identical to claiming intimate decisions are protected by "liberty of action." Furthermore, the rubric "liberty of action" has the advantage of historical precedent. Assuming, as does Gavison, that matters of regulating access are at the conceptual core of privacy, matters that are conceptually distinct from liberty of action (since they involve duties of noninterference on the part of others), we merely muddy the theoretical waters by speaking of privacy with respect to intimate decisions. Thus, although we should retain intimate access for privacy's content, we should exclude decisional matters as best belonging within the sphere of liberty of action.

The argument that we should abandon constitutional privacy on the grounds that it is nothing more than liberty of action is initially plausible. After all, even cursory consideration shows that the intimate decisions protected by constitutional privacy delineate a realm of liberty of action. For example, if I have a privacy right to control my childbearing, I can also be said to possess liberty of action with respect to childbearing. Similarly, if I have a privacy right to control my sexual expression in most situations, I can also be said to possess liberty of action with respect to my sexuality. Despite its initial plausibility, the argument that attempts to dissolve decisional privacy into liberty of action suffers from three flaws. First, it does not provide a defense against the argument that decisional/constitutional privacy involves liberties that possess a feature distinguishing them from nonprivacy liberties. Second, it offers no explanation of how we have come to confuse privacy and liberty of action. Third, if we accept this argument, it also undermines access-based privacy theories, pulling the rug out from under itself. Let me expand upon these points. According to the first criticism, the link between constitutional privacy and liberty of action can be interpreted in two ways—as indicating that decisional privacy is a confused concept or as pointing to something distinctive about privacy-protected liberty of action. Given that we *do* distinguish between privacy-invoking liberty of action and liberty of action not protected by privacy, surely it is more plausible to seek the basis for this distinction than to abandon it as confused. Turning to the second criticism, we possess no particular reason to believe that we have indeed confused liberty of action with decisional privacy—Ruth Gavison's argument lacks any explanation of the birth of our "confusion." Finally, if we were to accept her argument (in the spirit of Ockham), our razor would cut too far for the access theorist. Although constitutional privacy most clearly covers certain liberties, the same can be said of access-based definitions of privacy; for example, if I have a privacy claim to control access to myself, thus limiting a peeping Tom's access, I can also be said to have a certain liberty, namely, the liberty to exercise this control. Thus, if we reject decisional privacy because of its tie to liberty, we also have grounds to reject access-control definitions of privacy. Given the centrality of access regulation to privacy, we have every reason to reject an argument that leads to its abandonment. Faced with these criticisms, a privacy theorist cannot abandon decisional privacy by merely linking it to liberty of action.

Once again, we are faced with a quandary. Changing privacy's content from intimate information to intimate access has its advantages. By so doing, we retain intimate information (in the guise of informational access) within the scope of privacy, while broadening privacy's scope to include noninformational intimate access. Nevertheless, this change does not help us when we are faced with privacy that involves protecting an agent's intimate decisions about her own actions; these decisions cannot be compressed into access matters. Yet the tie between an individual's intimate decisions about her actions and privacy has resisted criticism. Therefore, explaining privacy's content in terms of access does not encompass its entire content. How are we to resolve the apparently conflicting demands of decisional and access privacy?

An agent's intimate decisions about her own actions seem to be inescapably within the domain of privacy. Yet matters of intimate access also seem to be within this domain. There are two ways in which the conflict between these apparently disparate aspects of privacy can be resolved. First of all, intimate access can be rejected as part of privacy; privacy involves *only* control over intimate decisions about an individual's own actions. Second of all, both intimate access and intimate decisions can be included within privacy's content by offering an explanation of what ties together these disparate areas. In what follows, I argue that explaining privacy's content only in terms of an agent's intimate decisions about her actions is unsatisfactory since matters of intimate access and informational access also fall within privacy's domain, but including intimate access and an agent's intimate decisions about her actions within privacy's content is satisfactory. The factor tying together these seemingly disparate areas of privacy is their intimacy.

Given the apparent dissimilarity between an agent's intimate decisions about her actions and questions of intimate access, it is tempting to "explain" this dissimilarity by simply excluding intimate access from the content of privacy. This is not an uncommon path to follow; constitutional privacy cases never explain how decisional privacy relates to tort law (access) privacy, leaving the impression that decisional privacy is "true" privacy. This impression is strengthened when we turn to the work of several theorists who have commented on constitutional privacy. These privacy theorists attempt to provide a coherent theoretical framework for constitutional privacy, but they neglect to provide a framework large enough to include matters of intimate access.[33] However, can access matters simply be removed from the scope of privacy, given their prevalence within the field of privacy? Certainly not without an argument; but the only plausible one has previously proven to be unsuccessful. We could reverse the "liberty argument" provided by access theorists against decisional privacy (in other words, control over intimate access could be described as a matter of liberty, and hence, not a privacy issue), but this reversal would fall victim to the criticisms I directed at it in its original form. Barring this move, intimate access issues cannot be removed from the content of privacy, due to their . prevalence in ordinary linguistic usage and tort law, and our lack of any reason to think that this prevalence is based on confusion.

There remains one final route: we must incorporate both intimate access to an agent and an agent's intimate decisions about her own actions into the content of privacy. The obstacle standing in the way of this incorporation is the apparent lack of a conceptual tie between decisional and access privacy issues. Ruth Gavison believes that the lack of such an apparent tie entails a rejection of decisional privacy:

If the concepts we use give the appearance of differentiating concerns without in fact isolating something distinct, we are likely to fall victims to this false appearance and our chosen language will be a hindrance rather than a help. The reason for excluding [decisional privacy situations] is that they present precisely such a danger.[34]

Although Gavison's argument is designed to exclude decisional privacy, it can be reversed to exclude matters of access from privacy's content (assuming we reject Gavison's intuition that access matters are more basic to privacy than decisional matters). Either way, the crux of it remains the same—assimilating decisions about actions and access matters under the common heading of "privacy" represents a loss of conceptual focus.

Fortunately, after considering the nature of the decisions and matters of access that have been brought within the scope of privacy in this book, the force of this criticism is lost. I have *not* argued that all forms of access or decisions about actions are included in privacy's content. I have argued that *intimate* access and decisions about actions fall within privacy's domain. Hence, there is a conceptual focus uniting the decisional and access aspects of privacy—the shared focus on intimacy. Rather than seeing privacy as composed of two disparate elements, we should understand it as protecting a realm of intimacy, a realm that happens to have both access and liberty of action aspects. Given that intimacy is the "something distinct" about decisional and access privacy, Gavison's argument collapses.

Having argued that both an agent's intimate decisions about her own actions and intimate access to the agent (including intimate informational access) belong within privacy's content, I now wish to perform a curious backtrack. As I have previously indicated, many privacy theorists assume that there is an important structural distinction between decision and access-based privacy.[35] It is simple to see what underlies this assumption. On the one hand, privacy restrictions on intimate access (including intimate informational access) are primarily designed to give rise to duties of noninterference on the part of *others*. For example, when I seek privacy with respect to access to areas of my body, I seek to impose duties on others not to access my body without permission. On the other hand, the intimate decisional privacy issues protected by constitutional privacy law concern the *agent's* own intimate actions. For example, when I seek privacy with respect to my decisions about contraception, I am primarily concerned with possessing freedom of action with regard to my use of contraceptives. However, this division is not as distinct as it initially appears. Consider a privacy claim concerning a matter of intimate access, for example, with respect to being touched by others or with respect to having a diary read by others. In making such a claim, we do not seek to avoid all access by others; we seek control over *decisions* about intimate access to ourselves. We wish to be free to decide who may access us. Consider also a privacy claim concerning a matter of "decisional privacy," for example, concerning a decision about abortion or a decision about sexual activity with a consenting partner. Such claims are claims to have control over *decisions* concerning our intimate actions. We wish to be free to decide how to act with respect to intimate situations. In short, both "access" and "decisional" privacy claims are claims to have control over *decisions;* hence, the distinction between decision-based and access-based privacy collapses. Rather than understanding privacy's content in terms of intimate access *and* intimate decisions, we should draw together these seemingly disparate areas: privacy's content covers intimate decisions, including the agent's decisions concerning intimate access to herself (including informational access) and her decisions about her own intimate actions.[36] In the following chapters, my discussion of intimate decisions will cover both types of decision.

It may appear that I have provided all the pieces necessary for an adequate definition of privacy. Starting with the initial assumption that privacy provides the individual with control over certain aspects of her life, I have shown that the content of privacy includes our decisions about intimate informational access, intimate access, and our own intimate actions. The intimacy of these aspects of privacy constitutes the conceptual focus of privacy. Putting together these pieces, privacy can be defined as the state of an agent possessing control over a realm of intimacy, which includes her decisions about intimate informational access, intimate access, and intimate actions. Yet there remains a deficiency in this privacy definition: it depends upon the notion of intimacy, yet I have not defined intimacy. The next chapter supplies this definition.

Notes

1. Assuming that privacy works through control, an information-based definition of privacy would be "privacy is the state of possessing control over information about yourself." For examples of information-based definitions of

privacy, see Judith Jarvis Thomson, "The Right to Privacy," *Philosophy and Public Affairs* 4 (1975): 295–314; Charles Fried, "Privacy," *Yale Law Journal* 77 (1968): 475–93; Alan Westin, *Privacy and Freedom* (New York: Atheneum, 1967); Elizabeth Beardsley, "Privacy: Autonomy and Selective Disclosure," in *Privacy: Nomos XIII,* ed. J. Roland Pennock and John W. Chapman (New York: Atherton Press, 1971), 56–70; Richard Wasserstrom, "Privacy: Some Arguments and Assumptions," in *Philosophical Law,* ed. Richard Bronaugh (Westport, CT: Greenwood Press, 1978), 148–66.

2. Assuming that privacy functions through control, an access-based definition of privacy amounts to "privacy is the state of possessing control over access to your self." For examples of access-based privacy definitions, see Jeffrey Reiman, "Privacy, Intimacy and Personhood," *Philosophy and Public Affairs* 6 (1976): 26–44; James Rachels, "Why Privacy Is Important," *Philosophy and Public Affairs* 4 (1975): 323–33; Richard Parker, "A Definition of Privacy," *Rutgers Law Review* 27 (1974): 275–96; Thomas Scanlon, "Thomson on Privacy," *Philosophy and Public Affairs* 4 (1975): 315–22.

3. Assuming that privacy functions through control, a definition of privacy based on intimate decisions amounts to "privacy is the state of possessing control over the making and implementation of intimate decisions about your actions." For examples of intimate decision based privacy definitions, see Tom Gerety, "Redefining Privacy," *Harvard Civil Rights–Civil Liberties Law Review* 12 (1977): 233–96; June Eichbaum, "Towards an Autonomy-Based Theory of Constitutional Privacy: Beyond the Ideology of Familial Privacy," *Harvard Civil Rights–Civil Liberties Law Review* 14 (1979): 361–84; David A. J. Richards, "Unnatural Acts and the Constitutional Right to Privacy," *Fordham Law Review* 45 (1977): 1312–48.

4. Note that these labels are used only to accord with common usage in the privacy literature. Clearly, giving the agent control over information or access to herself can be described as giving her control over certain decisions. For the purposes of this chapter, decisional privacy is equivalent to constitutional privacy.

5. Information about the agent should not be narrowly construed; it can be information about her behavior, plans, or other aspects of her life.

6. The objection might be raised that I am describing a situation where privacy has been merely *lost,* not *violated.* Only if the person has gathered the information in a culpable manner should we take the additional step of describing the privacy loss as a privacy violation. I accept that a loss of privacy may not be a morally culpable violation; an agent might justifiably or simply inadvertently lessen the privacy of another. However, I believe that the term "violation" should be retained for both culpable and nonculpable cases of lessened privacy. This term makes it clear that we have a prima facie claim to privacy since privacy is a presumptive good; when someone lessens another's privacy, they violate her in a

way that demands explanation. If they offer a satisfactory explanation, they may avoid blame for their violation, yet the violation still remains real: by losing privacy, the agent has lost something of value to herself; she has been damaged, even if no one is held culpable for the damage.

7. This is understandable, given that tort privacy law is claimed to have developed due to a lawyer's desire to create a legal redress against the yellow journalism of his time. See Samuel Warren and Louis Brandeis, "The Right to Privacy," *The Harvard Law Review* 4 (1890): 193–220.

8. To illustrate this, consider California's Right to Privacy Law.

9. William A. Parent, "Recent Work on the Concept of Privacy," *American Philosophical Quarterly* 4 (1983): 343.

10. Alan Westin, *Privacy and Freedom* (New York: Atheneum, 1967), 7.

11. This fact overturns a number of information-based privacy definitions, such as Alan Westin's.

12. Though I focus this example on the revelation of sexual information, my argument covers other types of intimate information, such as information about my family life, love affairs, or inner thoughts.

13. Although I focus on information concerning a parking place, any number of informational alternatives could be substituted involving other instances of impersonal information dissemination, for example, my talkative friend could reveal my car's color, the nature of my job, or the timber of my voice.

14. This is not to suggest that information about a parking place is *necessarily* outside of the scope of privacy. It is to suggest that the burden of proof is on the agent to explain why information about her parking place is intimate.

15. Of course, we *could* contend that all information is private, including information about a parking place. I am willing to accept this modification, but it does nothing more than reword the privacy theorist's task—she still has to determine why certain types of information are "essentially private."

I do not mean to suggest that the boundary between intimate and nonintimate information is clear; it is not. For example, a nonintimate piece of information may become intimate strictly on the basis of where it is located: if I write about the weather in my personal journal, I can still justifiably claim that my privacy was invaded if another reads my weather report without permission.

16. This is not to suggest that all information about parties and employment is necessarily nonintimate; it is only to suggest that the vague information involved in my examples does not have the status of intimate information.

17. Compare this to my reaction upon being questioned about truly private information. If I were questioned by a stranger about my sex life, an exclamation of, "That's not something you should ask me about!" would constitute a satisfactory rejoinder.

18. For an example of this, see the Federal Privacy Act.

19. I could describe what took place in both the party and job information

example as a "privacy violation" without committing an obvious verbal error. Furthermore, my description would probably successfully convey my intended meaning, including its prescriptive aspect, i.e., the teller of the information told something she ought not to have told.

20. Though we can justify secrecy claims in many circumstances. We have an expansive property-based secrecy claim with respect to much nonintimate information; for example, clearly I have a justified secrecy claim to control my own information about the profitable computer technology I have been fortunate enough to develop, since it is my property. The Constitution's protection against nonintimate search and seizure partially acknowledges the importance of protecting secrecy claims with respect to property.

21. Morton Levine, "Privacy in the Tradition of the Western World," in *Privacy,* ed. William Bier (New York: Fordham University Press, 1980), 19.

22. Since this work focuses on privacy, I will not discuss secrecy at greater length. For further information about the relation between privacy and secrecy, see Sissela Bok, *Secrets: On the Ethics of Concealment and Revelation* (New York: Random House, 1983).

23. Assume that the victim hid sufficiently rapidly that the peeping Tom did not even learn where she had hidden, since this knowledge might be construed as an acquisition of information about the agent.

24. Scanlon, "Thomson on Privacy," 320.

25. See Rachels, "Why Privacy Is Important," 329; and Reiman, "Privacy, Intimacy and Personhood."

26. "Access to an individual" should be broadly construed. It should not be understood as involving only direct contact through the senses with the individual. We can also gain access through intermediary sources or even by merely entering into her "personal space." For example, reading someone's private journal without her permission would count as gaining access to the individual, as would learning a piece of information about her, which reveals the continuity between the information and access-based privacy accounts.

27. Note that this interpretation of access as including a subset of informational access will be accepted in the remainder of this work.

28. An access privacy theorist might respond that our intuitions are confused: someone glancing at a woman's hands *does* lessen her privacy in the same way as someone grabbing her breast since both actions involve uncontrolled access. Yet we still have to explain why certain access violations, such as breast grabbing, are so much more significant than others. The obvious answer would be that certain areas of the body, such as a woman's breasts, are "private," while others are not, but this does no more than restate the problem. The access theorist still has to explain why certain forms of access, intimate ones, are at the core of privacy.

29. See Bowers v. Hardwick, minority opinion, 85 U.S. 140 (1986).

30. See Bowers v. Hardwick, majority opinion.

31. Note that I use "constitutional privacy issues" as a synonym for decisional privacy with respect to our actions.

32. Ruth Gavison, "Privacy and the Limits of Law," in *Philosophical Dimensions of Privacy: An Anthology,* ed. Ferdinand Schoeman (New York: Cambridge University Press, 1984), 358.

33. For examples, see Eichbaum, "Towards an Autonomy-Based Theory of Constitutional Privacy"; and David A. J. Richards, *Toleration and the Constitution* (New York: Oxford University Press, 1986).

34. Gavison, "Privacy and the Limits of Law," 357.

35. For example, see Gavison, "Privacy and the Limits of Law."

36. The reason why I avoided grouping together "decisional" and "access" privacy is that this move would have abandoned the divisions commonly found in privacy theory and failed to simplify the task at hand. The problem of linking together an agent's decisions about informational access, noninformational access, and intimate actions would have remained in need of a solution.

6

Intimacy: The Core of Privacy

Why do my decisions about revealing the contents of my diary fall within the scope of privacy? Why do we have a privacy interest in making our own decisions about whom we kiss or allow to kiss us? Why do many decisions about consenting sexual expression fall within the domain of privacy? Assuming that privacy protects a realm of intimacy for the agent, the initial answer to these questions is clear: these decisions are protected by privacy because they are intimate. However, this response simply leads to a new question: what constitutes an intimate decision? We might reply that decisions are intimate when they concern intimate matters, unfortunately, this response simply moves the locus of the problem—we still need to know why the acts and activities regulated by intimate decisions are themselves intimate.[1] Specifically, we need to explain the intimacy of certain instances of physical access to a person, certain instances of informational access to a person, and certain activities a person might undertake, such as motherhood, friendship, and marriage.[2] There are two directions in which we may proceed in our attempt to locate the characteristic that makes certain acts and activities intimate. First, from what I will term a "behaviorist" direction, we might find some characteristic of the behavior constituting intimate acts and activities that could identify them as intimate (hence decisions about these matters are intimate). Second, in motivational terms, we might find some aspect of the motivations demanded by certain acts and activities that could identify them as intimate (hence decisions about these matters are intimate).[3] In this chapter, I show that there is nothing about the behavior constituting intimate acts and activities that identifies them as intimate. Instead, intimate decisions are identified by their motivation-dependent content. When an agent characterizes an act or activity as

74

intimate, she is claiming that it draws its meaning and value from her love, liking, or care. Intimate decisions concern such matters and, thus, involve a choice on the agent's part about how to (or not to) embody her love, liking, or care.

It may initially appear obvious that the source of the intimacy of various acts and activities is the behavior that constitutes them. The appeal of this possibility lies in that it refers to something readily identified—behavior. This straightforward behaviorist characterization of intimacy corresponds with our ordinary intuition that intimate matters are not difficult to identify; for example, upon seeing two people kissing, the act is rapidly categorized as "intimate." If we were asked to justify this categorization, we might respond by indicating the behavior once again, "Can't you see what they're doing?" Certain acts and activities appear to be intimate simply by virtue of the instance or type of behavior involved; for example, we might contend that acts and activities involving sexual behavior are intimate merely by virtue of involving sexual behavior. Despite this initial appeal, I believe that neither particular instances nor general types of behavior are in essence intimate; locating intimacy in some feature of behavior fails to accord with the nature of intimacy claims.

Let us consider whether particular examples of behavior might be intrinsically intimate. This possibility encounters one overwhelming objection: it is impossible to explain how a particular instance of behavior could, *qua* behavior, have an inherently intimate "essence." For example, consider someone kissing another. Clearly intimate in many instances in our society, it is perfectly conceivable that this could be otherwise. In another culture or historical period, the behavior that constitutes kissing another might be equivalent to a nonintimate gesture such as tapping someone on the shoulder—people might kiss others merely in order to gain their attention. Faced with this different culture or historical period, it would be absurd to suggest that kissing retains its intimacy—despite the fact that kissing *qua* behavior remains the same. To highlight this absurdity, consider a scenario: a member of a different society visits our society, only to be horrified at our habit of tapping others on the shoulder to gain their attention. She explains that that action is considered intimate in her society. Since the gesture is identical behavior in each society, she prescribes to us that tapping others on the shoulder *should* be considered intimate in our society. Clearly we would dispute her prescription, but we would not contest the fact that the behavior involved was the same in her society and our own. Rather, we might point out that the gesture does not mean the same thing in each society and, hence, does not retain its intimacy in our society. The point emerging from this example is that particular instances of behavior clearly lack an intimate essence; otherwise, we could not accommodate the fact that intimacy is not static across time or culture.

The behaviorist argument need not be that *particular* instances of behavior, such as kissing another, are inherently intimate. The behaviorist may field a different argument: general classes or types of behavior, such as sexual behavior, are inherently intimate. When we seek to identify intimate behavior across cultures or historical periods, we should look for the culture or time-specific instances of behavior that embody the intrinsically intimate general class of behavior. For example, if we assume that sexual behavior is the intimate general class, in one culture sexual behavior may take the form of kissing, while in another culture it may take the form of tapping people on the shoulder. This move may temporarily save the behaviorist argument from being set aside, but not for long. It is simple to find an example that undermines the idea of the inherent intimacy of general classes of behavior by looking at our own society. For example, the claim for the class of sexual behavior is overturned by considering the behavior of people performing sex acts for financial gain. Similarly, an argument that child-rearing behavior is essentially intimate would collapse when faced with child abuse. In such cases, merely pointing at the behavior exhibited and exclaiming, "That's intimate!" carries no power to convince—nothing in the nature of the behavior forces us to acknowledge its intimacy. As this example demonstrates, general classes of behavior are no more necessarily intimate than was the case with particular instances of behavior such as kissing.

I have shown that instances or classes of behavior cannot be classified as necessarily intimate, yet my behaviorist opponent is not inescapably committed to behavior being in essence intimate or nonintimate. She is free to argue that behavior must be identified as intimate with reference to its social context; for example, intimate behavior might be behavior that is self-regarding. Nevertheless, even this context-dependent approach cannot overcome a final problem that faces the entire behaviorist project: intimacy claims are put forward prior to and without regard for considerations of behavior. Consider such intimate matters as kissing another and friendship. When we claim that these matters are intimate, we do not establish these claims by specifying the behavior they involve; we do not indicate that a friendship will involve taking another to the movies, talking with her, and so forth. We discuss the rationale of these activities, pointing to the fact that they demand *more* from us than mere behavior. Yet if intimacy were a product of behavior, a specification of behavior would be exactly the path to follow to justify these claims. The fact that intimacy claims can be made without a description of behavior leads to the conclusion that the behaviorist has mistakenly focused on behavior; intimacy stems from something prior to behavior.

If it is not behavior that marks certain acts and activities as intimate, what about the agent's motivations? Perhaps some determinate aspect of the motivations demanded by those acts and activities identifies them as intimate. In what follows, I point out that many acts and activities do not require any particular motivation from the agent; this is because their meaning and value are understood in terms of considerations external to the agent's motivations. However, not all are of this sort; to call an act or activity "intimate" is to claim it is *not* of this sort, but draws its meaning and value from the agent's love, liking, or care.

On initial consideration, the idea of linking the intimacy of certain acts and activities to the motivations they demand from the agent seems implausible. After all, many acts and activities demand no particular motivation on the agent's part; they can fulfill their purposes regardless of the agent's motivations. Consider the action of going to the grocery store. Though it may be pleasant or even desirable for me to undertake this action under the influence of a particular motivation, questions about my motivation seem readily separable from the action of going to the store. If my roommate were to say, "You must go to the grocery store, we are out of food," it would be ludicrous for me to respond, "My motivation is faulty, so I can't." If I were to respond in this fashion, my roommate might reply, "You can get to the store quite satisfactorily despite your motivations!" In this case, my roommate considers my response ludicrous because the grocery decision concerns an act—going to the store—that is not commonly understood as dependent on the agent's motivations. If I were to perform this act with any variety of motivations, my action could still attain its end—new groceries at home. Trips to the grocery store can fulfill their purpose with any variety of motivations on the agent's part because this purpose is defined in terms of factors external to the agent. Consider the action of brushing teeth. It may be pleasant to do this under the influence of certain motivations, but the nature of this action does not inherently require any given motivation. If the state were to rule that all citizens must brush their teeth, we might argue that such decisions are best left to individual citizens since the government is incompetent to regulate teeth brushing, but we would not argue that its meaning and value would be damaged if the state forced this action upon citizens as it requires a motivation that cannot be forced. We would not offer this argument because the meaning and value of teeth brushing derive from considerations external to the agent's motivations. Brushing teeth is a means to attain an end—clean teeth, and value is accorded to the action in proportion to the value accorded this end. As long as the meaning and value of teeth brushing are understood to lie in such external ends, the nature of this pursuit does not require reference to the agent's motivations. To generalize the points that emerge from these examples, the meaning and value of acts and activities can be understood to stem from considerations external to the agent, such as the attainment of a particular end, efficacy, the good of society, and so forth. If the meaning and value of an act or activity derive from such external considerations, the agent's motivation is extrinsic to them.

The fact that many acts and activities draw their meaning and value from considerations that have nothing to do with the agent's motivations does not entail that all matters must be characterized in isolation from the agent's motivation. Let us consider how such intimate matters as showing others love letters, allowing a kiss, and raising a child can be understood as drawing their meaning and value from the agent's motivation. In what follows, I suggest that seeing these matters as intimate involves understanding them as drawing their value and meaning from the agent's love, care, or liking.

Before I plunge into my discussion of the ties between intimacy and love, care, and liking, let me put forward an important caveat about my discussion of these emotions. Even my initial mention of the agent's love, liking or care has probably been sufficient to raise questions in your minds, leading you to scribble questions in this book's margins. What constitutes true liking, love, and care? How are we to distinguish between these emotions? As these questions reveal, it is obvious that my account of privacy demands a theory of emotion, especially a theory of love, care, or liking—a theory of affection. However, though I suggest directions such a theory might take, I do not provide a thorough account of emotion in this work, and therefore need to provide a few stipulative qualifications to my discussion of love, liking, and care. As I will use these terms, they refer to emotions that exist between people; although we may talk about a person "loving" candy, I believe this is not a genuine case of love. Furthermore, the emotions of care, liking, and love are potentially constitutive of specific forms of relationships, relationships characterized by considerations such as consent, fairness, and mutuality. These assumptions in place, let us turn to the issue of intimacy.

Consider the intimate gesture of showing another one's love letters. Clearly the intimacy of this action is not necessarily a function of their content; were they nothing more than mundane details about our lives, showing them to another could still amount to an intimate act. If it is not the content of love letters that figures in their intimacy, the intimacy of displaying them must result from the function such a gesture serves (or is assumed to serve) for the agent. What meaning is conveyed when we show our love letters to another? It conveys that the other person stands in a special relation to us, that we care for, like, or love the other person. Not only is the meaning of the love letter gesture tied to our motivation, the value we accord to it is also motivation dependent: we value showing another our love letters because we value expressing our liking, care, or love to that person. Others accord value to being shown the letters because they, too, understand the action to express our care, liking, or love. Hence, the act of showing another our love letters draws its meaning and value as an *intimate act* from its tie to our love, liking, or care.

A similar argument holds in the case of the intimate act of allowing ourselves to be kissed. As I have argued, there is nothing in the behavior itself that explains its intimacy. But consider the role played by kissing in our society. In much of our society, kissing another is not equivalent to a nonintimate gesture such as tapping them on the shoulder, the difference lying in the source of the meaning and value accorded to the gesture. The meaning of allowing a kiss is tied to the agent's motivation (in most cases),[4] drawn from its role in expressing the agent's care, liking, or love for another. The tie between allowing a kiss and the agent's motivation is also the source of the value accorded to kissing, usually seen as an expression of our feeling rather than as a merely physical action. The meaning and value accorded to such an act depends on the agent's emotional motivation; the act of allowing a kiss draws its intimacy from this dependency.

The activity of mothering seems different from sharing love letters or allowing a kiss.[5] Mothering is a form of life, not a mere gesture.

However, consider the meaning and value we attach to it. Motherhood is obviously characterized by certain general ways of behaving—bearing a child, feeding the child, dressing the child, and so forth—but this behavior embodies motherhood in merely the biological sense of perpetuating the species.[6] There is also the intimate "moral or personal sense" of motherhood. In its moral sense it makes demands not only on the mother's behavior, but also on her feelings—specifically, the mother's love, liking, or care for the child. Motherhood in the moral sense supposes that the mother's motivation in raising a child is love, not duty or necessity. When we see a mother caring for a child, we understand her actions to mean that she loves the child, not that she is seeking some external end. This element of love not only informs the meaning of the mother's behavior, but also the distinctive value accorded to the behavior. If we learned a mother were raising a child motivated only by a desire to win a prize, clearly we would think that her "motherhood" was missing something of value—affection for the child. The activity of mothering is dependent on the agent's love to give it meaning and value. Hence, the connection between the intimacy of showing another love letters, allowing a kiss, and mothering is clear: these activities draw their meaning and value from the agent's love, liking, or care.

Having argued that showing another one's love letters, allowing a kiss, and raising a child are intimate matters because they are understood to draw their meaning and value from the agent's love, liking, or care, my argument is open to the criticism that these matters *can* be understood in terms of other considerations. We might intend to make money by allowing ourselves to be kissed or displaying my love letters; the value we accord to these matters might be proportional to the money we hope to receive. Similarly, we might mean to help the state by raising a child; the value we accord to the action might stem from the achievement of this end. Doesn't this suggest that the intimacy of these matters stems from a different source than the agent's motivations? I accept that allowing ourselves to be kissed, showing love letters to another, and child raising can be characterized in terms that do not refer to the actor's love, liking, or care, but all this indicates is that they are not necessarily intimate. If we were to understand kissing, displaying love letters, and child raising exclusively in such terms, our interpretations of these actions would have relinquished their intimacy. If we fail to link both the meaning and the value of our actions to love, liking, or care, we have divorced our actions from intimacy. If I meant to express love through a kiss, yet I only valued my kiss because I expected a financial reward, I would not understand it as intimate. If I meant to antagonize others by showing them my love letters, valuing such a display only in proportion to the antagonism it elicited, I would not understand my display as intimate. Although we *can* characterize any supposedly intimate matter in terms of considerations external to ourselves, by so doing we reveal that we no longer understands it as intimate.

Showing another one's love letters, allowing a kiss, and mothering are intimate because they draw their meaning and value from the agent's love, liking, or care[7]; hence, decisions about them are intimate because of their intimate subject matter. However, these isolated examples do not decisively establish my argument: they only provide its initial motivation. The next question is whether my arguments about these cases can be generalized to intimate access, intimate informational access, and the activities protected by constitutional privacy law.[8]

The intimacy of information stems from the role the information plays for the agent, specifically the role the information plays for the agent when she conveys it to others.[9] This role may refer to the information's content (e.g., sexual information may play a particular role for the agent), but the content is subordinated to the role. Ferdinand Schoeman provides an important clue as to the nature of this role by pointing out that intimate "information is to be regarded as special and thus only revealed in certain contexts—contexts in which the very giving of the information is valued as a special act."[10] What feature of the act of conveying certain information to another makes it a "special act"? When we tell another about the deaths in the family, incidents in our love lives, or our innermost thoughts, the action of conveying this information usually indicates more than simply a desire on our part to inform the person. The fact that we are telling the other person these facts, facts we understand as personal, conveys something about our relation to the person, usually that we are in, or seek to be in, a close relationship with that person. There are two ways in which the action of information sharing can play this special role.

First of all, there is Charles Fried's "commodity theory" of intimacy: information is intimate when it functions as a commodity from which relationships can be constructed. Fried argues that close relationships

involve the voluntary and spontaneous relinquishment of *something* between friend and friend, lover and lover. The title to information about oneself conferred by privacy provides the necessary something. . . . intimacy is the sharing of information about one's actions, beliefs, or emotions which one does not share with all, and which one has the right not to share with anyone.[11]

The act of sharing information with another is intimate when that being shared is a scarce, restricted commodity.

Fried's suggestion is interesting and insightful, yet it stops short of capturing the core of intimacy. On the one hand, his account provides a promising starting point; intimate information *does* seem to be somehow constitutive of close relationships. A close relationship finds expression in a context of mutually shared communication, which is often restricted to the participants in the relationship alone; in fact, an initial account of intimate information might be "information I only tell my friends." It is difficult to imagine characterizing a relationship as "close" if it lacked this context; the very lack of shared information seems to preclude the possibility of a close relationship. On the other hand, sharing information with another might be a necessary condition for intimacy, but not sufficient by itself. If it were, many of us would have closer relationships with our doctors than our friends, assuming that doctors usually possess more restricted information than do friends. Similarly, by sharing information about my car with my mechanic (information known by few), I would be building an intimate relationship. Clearly both of these claims are incorrect—sharing scarce information with a doctor or mechanic does not necessarily build intimacy. Furthermore, when we share information in this fashion, we do not mean to convey merely its regulated nature—we feel no need to inform our friend that no one else possesses the information we are sharing. Neither do we value our act merely because we view the information as a limited commodity—the value we accord to the information is not explained by, "That's not something I tell to everyone, so it's special!" Given these challenges to Fried's account, we are left wondering how the sharing of information builds close relationships, assuming that the context of scarcity does not explain alone this link. What sort of significance must be imbued in information if it is to be constitutive of close relationships?

The second possibility emerged in my love letter example; the context that provides the act of conveying information the status of a "special act" is one of care, liking, or love. When we tell someone personal information about ourselves, including information we have not told to others, we mean to convey our care, liking, or love for the person. Without these emotions underlying our act, we would understand it as without intimate meaning. If the individual to whom we were disclosing the information understood its factual content satisfactorily, but not its expression of caring, liking, or loving, we would feel that our act was worthless *as an intimate act*—our message would have misfired. Not only is the meaning we attach to our act of information sharing dependent on our love, liking, or care, so is its value. If we valued conveying this meaning only because it produced some extrinsic end, we would not be valuing the information as intimate. For example, if we valued showing our love letters to others, thus conveying the meaning that we cared for them, only so that we could extort money from them, we would not be valuing it as an intimate act. The act of sharing information, either actively or passively, is intimate if and only if it is understood to take its meaning and value from our love, liking, or care.

The intimacy of access also stems from the role the access serves for the agent, specifically the role it serves when she allows (or does not allow) the access to others. When an agent either passively or actively grants access to herself to another, her gesture indicates something about the relationship, as when we allow another to kiss us or see us undressed, or when we actively kiss another or display ourselves undressed. The fact that we are allowing access that we *understand* as significant and personal suggests that we share, or wish to share, a close relationship with the other. It might be proposed here, as was proposed for information sharing, that the act of allowing access is intimate simply because the access being allowed is a restricted commodity, not allowed to everyone. Thus, intimate access would be constitutive of close relationships because the individual who was allowed access would understand its restricted nature. This suggestion fails for the same reasons it failed in the case of information—access may be a necessary condition for intimacy, but it is not a sufficient one. It is a context of liking, caring, or loving that makes the act relevant to intimacy. When we provide intimate access to another, the meaning of our act flows from our emotions. For example, showing a diary to others is intimate because we show our diaries to those we love; kissing another is intimate because we kiss as a sign of care; allowing another to see our bedroom is intimate because I allow this as a gesture of affection. Without these or related emotions underlying my act, it would lack meaning as an intimate act.

Not only must the meaning of an intimate act flow from my love, liking, or care, its value must stem from the same source. If access is to be considered intimate, its value must also be seen as dependent on the agent's love, liking, or care. We value allowing intimate access to someone because we value expressing our care, liking, or love to that person. If we valued conveying this meaning only because it produced some extrinsic end, we would not be valuing it as intimate. For example, if I valued allowing another to enter my bedroom, thus conveying the meaning that I cared for the person, only so that I could play a harmless joke, this value would indicate that I did not understand the act as intimate, despite the meaning I was attempting to convey. Drawing together this point with my earlier one, we now have a complete account of what it means for an access to be intimate: it must be understood to draw its meaning and value from our love, liking, or care.

I have discussed how both the agent's passive act of allowing either physical or informational access and her engaged action of acceding access draw their intimacy from the fact that they are understood to derive their meaning and value from the agent's emotional stance. However, there still remains a problem: we often think of certain activities as inherently intimate without considering the intimate access they might involve. This point is readily illustrated by considering the activities protected by constitutional privacy law due to their intimacy: child rearing, family relationships, procreation, life in the home, marriage, contraception, and abortion.[12] What marks these constitutionally protected activities as intimate? To answer this question, let us consider the Court's rationale.

It is difficult to initially see how such activities can *all* be grouped together under the heading of intimacy. After all, focusing on the behavioral content of these activities produces a heterogeneous collection. However, the Supreme Court has focused on the role these activities play in the life of the individual. Consider its explanation of the intimacy of marriage: "Marriage is a coming together for better or for worse, hopefully enduring, and intimate to the degree of being sacred. It is an association that promotes a way of life, not causes; a harmony in living, not political faiths; a bilateral loyalty."[13] In other words, the activity of marriage is intimate because it possesses a special meaning and value in the agent's life. Similarly, abortion and contraceptive access are understood as intimate "because parenthood alters so dramatically an individual's self-definition, not because of demographic considerations."[14] Abortion and contraceptive use are understood as intimate because they regulate an activity (parenthood) that plays a special role in the agent's life. Finally, the Court sees family activities as intimate because they contribute "so powerfully to the happiness of individuals, not because of a preference for stereotypical households."[15] Once again, the intimacy of family activities lies in the role they play for the agent. There are two points to draw from these examples. First of all, constitutional privacy protects the activities constitutive of certain relationships (e.g., marriage, parenthood, family relations) and the actions that regulate those relationships (e.g., it protects decisions about abortion and contraception because these decisions concern matters that regulate parenthood).[16] Second of all, constitutional privacy protects these activities because the relationships are presumed to have a special significance in the agent's life. But what is this significance?

The clearest indication is found in two statements made by the Court. In *Roberts v. United States Jaycees,* the Court suggests that intimate activities embody the fact that we all depend on the "emotional enrichment of close ties with others."[17] In the dissenting opinion to *Bowers v. Hardwick,* Justice Blackmun suggests that intimate activities regulate the nature of an agent's personal associations with others.[18] Given these hints, let us consider how such activities as marriage, family affairs, motherhood, and child rearing regulate our ties to others. The first possibility is that they function in a manner described by Fried's commodity theory of intimacy—they are intimate activities because they are restricted. Thus, intimacy is the sharing of restricted activities with another, activities we do not share with all. But, once again, this account of intimacy places the cart before the horse. While intimate activities do seem to build relationships, they do not build relationships simply due to their restricted nature. The fact that we do not engage in the activities peculiar to marriage, the family, and friendship with all, for example, does not in itself establish intimacy or close ties with others when we engage in these restricted activities with them.[19] Additionally, this account of intimacy fails to explain the importance of the connection found by the Court between "emotional enrichment" and intimacy; restricted activities clearly have no necessary link to emotional enrichment simply *qua* restricted activities.

This leads to my second possibility—these activities may regulate our relationships with others by regulating our emotional ties, specifically the ties of love, liking, and care. For example, parenting "alters so dramatically an individual's self-definition" in part because it calls upon the agent not merely to act, but to love.[20] Family relationships contribute "so powerfully to the happiness of individuals" because they involve care.[21] Marriage promotes a "harmony in living" and "bilateral loyalty" because of the potential for love between the partners involved.[22] Insofar as marriage, family relations, and parenting are understood as intimate, both their meaning and value is dependent on the agent's love, liking, or care. If our understanding of the meaning and value of these activities should change—perhaps we become convinced that these activities embody nothing more than the spirit of capitalism and their value is dependent on the goals of capitalism—we would no longer understand them as intimate.

I have argued that interpreting acts of allowing access (including informational access), actions of giving access (including informational access), and constitutional privacy matters as intimate amounts to understanding them as drawing their meaning and value from the agent's love, liking, or care. When the agent no longer links the meaning and value of such matters to her love, liking, or care, she no longer understands these matters as intimate. This account of intimacy undermines the intuition noted earlier, namely, that intimacy is readily identified from an external point of view. According to my account, determinations of intimacy require the personal point of view, a view for which the agent holds an epistemologically privileged standpoint. If the agent's motivations are central to intimacy, then the external point of view is not an epistemologically privileged standpoint when it comes to making intimacy judgments. Consider an agent and an external observer discussing the intimacy of a particular act of the agent's; if the observer claimed, "I *know* that act draws its meaning and value from your love," we would turn to the *agent* for confirmation. If asked to justify our appeal to the agent, we might respond, "She's in the best position to know such things!" The agent's point of view assumes an epistemologically superior position with respect to the determination of intimacy—we assume that the personal point of view is the most accurate one from which to make judgments of motivations.[23] Even when an external observer makes an intimacy claim, the priority of the personal point of view over the external one still holds. If an observer were asked to judge whether or not a homosexual's sexual activities merited the description "intimate," it would be incorrect for her to automatically state that she "knew" such activities were not dependent on love, care, or liking for their meaning and value since the activities failed to correspond to the activities she personally viewed as expressions of love, care, or liking.[24] An external point of view provides no omniscient link to the agent's motivations. Faced with this difficulty, the observer must attempt to conceptually assume another's point of view, to stand in her shoes. The point of this argument is clear: the personal point of view—not the impersonal, external point of view—is the standpoint to assume to identify intimacy. Hence, describing an agent's act, action, or activity as drawing its meaning and value from her love, liking, or care is to make a claim about its significance from the agent's point of view. When society claims that something derives its meaning and value from the agent's love, liking, or care, society means that *people* commonly identify it as drawing its significance from their love, liking, or care. When an agent claims that something derives its meaning and value from her love, liking, or care, she means that its significance from her point of view stems from these emotions.

By constructing intimacy from the personal point of view and by allocating the agent epistemological priority, I may seem to impose no boundaries on the matters that can be construed as intimate. After all, an agent can claim that *any* of her acts, actions, or activities draws its meaning and value from her loving, caring, or liking, so all of her acts and activities are potentially intimate. Although I accept the validity of this argument, it collapses as a criticism. It is true that no acts or activities are *necessarily* excluded from the domain of intimacy; it is logically possible that an agent might understand any of her acts or activities as deriving its significance from her loving, caring, or liking. But several factors enable my argument to avoid unfettered relativism with respect to intimacy. First, the personal point of view is a social construct and, hence, will usually reflect the dominant social understanding of intimacy. Second, the agent faces a burden of proof to establish her intimacy claims. Third, the primacy of the personal point of view does not undermine the possibility that the agent's self-knowledge with respect to her emotions might be fallible. Fourth, since the attitudes of love, liking, and care are directed toward the development of affiliations with others, such as friendship, we can always criticize a person's claims about such states by contending that her actions do not support these affiliations.

Agents typically will not make unrestrained intimacy claims; any contention to the contrary does not pay sufficient attention to the fact that the personal point of view is itself a social construct. We need only think of the meaning and value attached to such activities as kissing another, marriage, sexual activity with a consenting partner, and family matters to realize that there is a substantial core of agreement about intimacy in our society. By living in this society, we tend to assimilate this accepted core into our personal point of view; for example, kissing is intimate from my point of view, but only because I have been socialized to understand it as an intimate act. Because our personal point of view is a product of society, the intimacy claims made from that point of view will largely reflect the understandings of society.

Of course, the fact that the personal point of view is a social construct does not entail that intimacy claims will *always* correspond with social norms. This leads to my second point: when an agent does make an intimacy claim that fails to accord with shared social understandings, both society and the agent are faced with a burden of proof. Due to the fact that the agent's intimacy claims stem from the personal point of view, she holds an epistemologically privileged position over society at large. Hence, society will always have to start by assuming the larger burden of proof when it seeks to undermine the agent's intimacy claims. However, the agent also has a burden of proof. This burden can be more or less difficult to shift, depending on the social context. For example, imagine a homosexual person arguing that her consenting homosexual activity with her partner draws its meaning and value from her love (and, hence, decisions about it are intimate). Given that heterosexual activity is commonly understood in these terms, the burden of proof for this claim seems relatively light (the main burden resting on those who would start by disproving it). Yet, if an agent claimed that the action of seat-belt fastening derived its meaning and value from her love, the burden of proof would weigh heavily on the agent, given the unusual nature of her claim. In short, simply *claiming* that a matter derives its significance from love, liking, or care does not automatically make it (and decisions concerning it) intimate. When society provides an argument against an intimacy claim, the person seeking to establish the claim must proceed to justify it against a social background.[25]

Third, accepting both that intimacy claims are constructed on the personal point of view and that the agent has privileged access to that point of view does not entail that intimacy claims are immune from criticism. It suggests that her intimacy claims have to be given greater weight than the claims of external parties; as I have shown, the burden of proof initially lies on the critics of the agent's claims. However, the agent's epistemologically privileged position with respect to her emotional motivations is neither infallible not inaccessible to others. Consider a wife batterer expressing his thoughts to a psychologist. This psychologist might lead him to realize that an activity he formerly understood as intimate, wife battering, was actually an expression of rage—his previous self-knowledge about his motivations was fallible. In such a case, the batterer's intimacy claims with respect to battering would clearly collapse; the batterer now would deny that his past actions expressed love for his partner. Such criticism on the part of the psychologist requires that she make a good faith attempt to understand the matter from the agent's point of view. If the psychologist truly wishes to respect intimacy, she ought not to immediately assume an external point of view and tell the batterer that it is obvious that his actions are not intimate simply due to their behavioral content. As psychology reveals, we do assume that it is possible to access and examine the motivations of others. Thus, an agent's intimacy claims can express her point of view without placing them beyond the reach of others.

But, we might object, many batterers continue to insist that their actions reveal love for their partner even after counseling; they *feel* the love. Similarly, many adults who sexually abuse children insist that their conduct reveals genuine love for the child; they argue that they unquestionably feel love. If these individuals apparently *feel* love, liking, or care, must we then accept that their behavior is intimate and, hence, privacy protected? If we assume that experiences of love, liking, or care are nothing more than sudden manifestations of ungoverned irrational feeling, we would be driven to accept that the batterer and child abuser might genuinely experience such states with reference to their victims. According to this description, experiences such as love, liking, and care would be little different from physical states such as being hot or cold; criticizing an agent's statement, "I'm acting from love," would be as difficult as challenging her claim, "I feel hot."

However, are emotional states such as care, love, and liking merely physiological? Are such states immune from judgment and critique? I think not. Care, love, and liking are more closely linked to virtues than to states of irrational feeling. Unlike an inherently individualistic claim about feeling hot, we identify these emotions by the characteristic ties to others they produce. In other words, they are not states of being that are conceptually private: they express themselves in their true forms in the formation of characteristic affiliations with others, such as friendship, mothering, fathering, and various forms of close partnership. These affiliations place certain demands on those involved, such as fairness, mutuality, and consent; we can criticize people for failing to meet these demands in their attachments to others. Now we can respond to the child abuser and wife batterer's claims about truly feeling love for their victims. Love is not identified strictly in terms of a passionate feeling; love is linked to the affiliations it supports.[26] But the child abuser's so-called love does not support an affiliation of friendship; true friendship is not compatible with such abuse, since the abuse denies the importance of consent to friendship. Similarly, the wife batterer's "love" does not support his affiliation with his wife; his behavior clearly violates the relationship constitutive norms of fairness, consent, and mutuality. Since neither the child abuser nor the wife batterer's "love" nurtures genuine attachments to others, we are justified in claiming that their experiences are not of true love. More generally, the personal point of view expressed in intimacy claims is constrained by the internal logic of affiliations. When an agent claims that something is intimate, she means that its significance from her point of view stems from the fact that it embodies *her* love, liking, or care; but the question of whether something embodies her *true* love, liking, or care cannot be answered by reference to a strictly private sensation—true love, liking, and care express themselves in the development of close affiliations with others that demand fairness, mutuality, and consent. Thus, neither an agent's claims about her love, liking, and care nor our own assessment of her emotions can be made in isolation from judgments about the nature of the attachments supported by the emotions.[27]

Let me summarize my circuitous discussion of intimacy. After assuming that intimate decisions are intimate because they concern intimate acts and activities, I revealed that the intimacy of these matters does not stem from behavior *qua* behavior. Rather, intimate matters draw their intimacy from their motivation dependency. An examination of a range of paradigmatic examples of intimate matters produced an account of intimate acts and activities: to claim that an act or activity is intimate is to claim that it draws its meaning and value from the agent's love, liking, or care. Intimate decisions concern such matters. Hence, they involve a choice on the agent's part about how to (or not to) embody her love, liking, or care. This account can be represented more formally:

Let Y = intimate decision about x.

Let x range over instances of access, instances of information dissemination, and the agent's activities.

To call *Y* "intimate" is to claim that it involves a choice on the agent's part about how to embody her love, care, or liking. *Y* involves such a choice because *x* draws its meaning and value from the agent's care, love, or liking.

Finally, I noted that the question of which matters are intimate cannot be settled from the impersonal point of view; claiming that a matter derives its meaning and value from the agent's emotional stance is to make a claim about the role it plays for the agent. Hence, the personal point of view cannot be separated from the determination of intimacy.

Having explained the nature of intimacy, how does it connect to my account of privacy? My previous definition of privacy defined privacy as "the state of the agent having control over intimate decisions, including decisions about access, information, and her actions." Given my account of intimacy, privacy now amounts to the state of the agent having control over decisions concerning matters that draw their meaning and value from the agent's love, caring, or liking. These decisions cover choices on the agent's part about access to herself, the dissemination of information about herself, and her actions. Since matters draw their meaning and value from the agent's love, liking, or care according to the role they play for the agent, the construction of intimacy lies on the agent's shoulders. Therefore, privacy claims are claims to possess autonomy with respect to our expression of love, liking, and care. For example, consider my claim to privacy with respect to my decisions about whether or not to kiss others. I want this control because I understand kissing as an action that derives its meaning and value from my love.[28] Hence, I want control over the expression of my love; my privacy claim amounts to a claim to possess such control.

A critic might argue that my account of privacy cannot be applied due to its dependency on the motivations that constitute intimacy—the courts and legislatures protect behavior, not motivations! This claim is correct to an extent: we can only generate and enforce laws that protect actions, but this does not mean that my account of privacy is useless. For the courts and legislatures, protecting privacy must take an indirect route. As motivations are opaque, protecting privacy entails protecting actions that are understood as expressions of love, care, or liking—even though these protected actions will not always be intimate. For example, we might include sexual activity between consenting, nonpaid partners within the scope of privacy laws, justifying this inclusion by pointing out that such activity commonly derives its meaning and value from the agents' affection for each other. Conversely, we might exclude paid prostitution from the scope of privacy laws, arguing that such paid activities commonly have little to do with the expression of affection. By making such divisions, we are not ruling out the possibility that certain agents may understand consenting sexual activity as merely an outlet for lust or that certain paid prostitutes may understand their work to be essential for developing affiliations based on their love, care, or liking. If these individuals *were* to appear and make their respective cases, the former would not be a justified privacy claim while the latter would. These divisions in the realm of lawmaking merely acknowledge that, since we cannot always know an agent's motivations, we must extend privacy over matters commonly understood to draw their meaning and value from the agent's love, liking, or care until we have evidence that this is not how the actor(s) understands them. We must exclude matters that are not understood to be dependent on the agent's affection until we have evidence that this is how the actor(s) understands them. Thus, my account of privacy can provide a foundation for laws and legal rulings, albeit ones that imperfectly cover intimacy.

Notes

1. An agent can express intimacy through either passive or active means. On the passive side, the agent can express intimacy by merely acceding access to another; for example, when I allow another to touch me (physical access) or to read my diary (informational access), my passive acts are intimate. On the active side, the agent can express intimacy by more kinetic means; for example, I can engage in activities such as sexual expression or motherhood to embody intimacy. For the purposes of this book, I will refer to the intimacy of "acts and activities" to recall to the reader's mind the passive and active aspects of intimacy. This is simply a stipulation on my part.

2. This is not a merely *ad hoc* division of intimacy; rather, it corresponds with the discussion of intimacy found in tort and constitutional privacy law. Tort privacy law focuses on protecting intimate access and intimate informational access; constitutional privacy law is concerned with intimate activities such as mothering, marriage, and family life. For further discussion of intimacy and privacy law, see David A. J. Richards, *Toleration and the Constitution* (New York: Oxford University Press, 1986).

3. The difference between these explanations is that the behaviorist explanation understands intimacy to lie in behavior *qua* behavior, while the motivational

account understands intimacy to lie in the motivations which find expression in behavior.

4. Even when allowing a kiss is merely an obligatory social greeting—e.g., allowing a disliked relative a kiss—it is still parasitic on the usual meaning and value we accord to a kiss as an expression of affection. We allow it because we wish the relative to believe that she is liked.

5. I focus on the issue of motherhood in this paragraph because I wish to account for the intimacy of a woman's decision to bear a child. However, my arguments can be generalized to both mothering and fathering.

6. In the biological sense, "motherhood" is a descriptive term, with no implications of intimacy.

7. Showing another love letters, kissing another, and mothering are, respectively, an instance of intimate information dissemination, an instance of intimate access, and an intimate activity of the type protected by constitutional privacy law.

8. As I attach the intimacy of information and access to the role that it plays for the agent when she accedes it to others—*either* through her own actions or through passively allowing access, clearly I am rejecting any account of intimacy that drives a conceptual wedge between the agent's active and passive contributions to intimacy. Hence, in what follows I focus on sharing information and access (*either* through one's actions or through passively allowing access) and the relationship-constitutive activities protected by constitutional law.

9. She may convey the information to others either actively (by telling others) or passively (by allowing others to learn it for themselves).

10. Ferdinand Schoeman, "Privacy and Intimate Information," in *Philosophical Dimensions of Privacy,* ed. Ferdinand Schoeman (New York: Cambridge University Press, 1984), 406.

11. Charles Fried, "Privacy," *Yale Law Journal* 77 (1968): 480.

12. See Carey v. Population Services International, 431 U.S. 678, 685 (1977) for a list of the cases which outline the reach of constitutional privacy claims.

13. Griswold v. Connecticut, 381 U.S. 479 (1965).

14. See Bowers v. Hardwick, dissenting opinion, 85 U.S. 140 (1986).

15. See Bowers v. Hardwick, dissenting opinion.

16. Hence, rather than determine why such actions as using contraception are intimate *qua* contraceptive use, we must determine why contraception is intimate *qua* the regulation of parenthood.

17. Roberts v. United States Jaycees, 468 U.S. 609 (1984). Note that Roberts v. United States Jaycees contains an explicit warning against limiting the scope of privacy to the family.

18. See Bowers v. Hardwick, dissenting opinion, section III.

19. If we were to encounter a parent who pursued the activities of being a parent motivated only by a desire to derive financial gain from her child, we might

reasonably protest that her parenting amounts to a mockery of intimacy. To justify this claim, rather than indicating the parent's behavior, we would attack her motivation as defective with respect to intimacy, "Look, she doesn't care for her child!"

20. Bowers v. Hardwick, dissenting opinion.

21. Bowers v. Hardwick, dissenting opinion.

22. Griswold v. Connecticut.

23. This is not to suggest that the personal point of view is infallible. As I will discuss, individuals can fail to fully understand their own motivations.

24. For an example of such a faulty move, see Bowers v. Hardwick. In this case, the majority opinion accepted that family activities, marriage, and procreation were intimate (and privacy protected), but rejected the idea that homosexual activity possessed any resemblance to these matters. In this decision, it is clear that the majority remained wedded to an external point of view with regard to its judgment about homosexual activities.

25. Someone might object that such a justification could not overcome the built-in assumptions of society. To illustrate that this is not necessarily the case, consider the practice of snake handling and the activities of certain religious groups. The activity of snake handling is not commonly understood to derive its meaning and value from the agent's belief. However, certain religious groups have successfully argued that the activity of snake handling does derive its meaning and value from such a source for their members.

26. Though I have no difficulty discarding the label "love" for the child abuser's feeling, someone else might wish to retain it. If this were the case, the distinction I draw here might be characterized as a distinction between the passion of love and the virtue of love, rather than as a distinction between love and its simulacra. In this book, I accept that true love, liking, and care are affiliation-producing emotions.

27. It is evident that my emotion-based account of intimacy depends upon a cognitivist account of the emotions, one capable of explaining how emotions can be judged. Although I cannot offer such an account within the constraints of this work, convincing cognitivist accounts are put forward by Alison Jaggar and Elizabeth Spelman. See Alison Jaggar, "Love and Knowledge: Emotion in Feminist Epistemology," in *Women, Knowledge, and Reality,* ed. Ann Garry and Marilyn Pearsall (Boston: Unwin Hyman, 1989): 129–55; and Elizabeth Spelman, "Anger and Insubordination," in Garry and Pearsall, *Women, Knowledge, and Reality,* 263–73.

28. Of course, my understanding of this action may be identical to that held by society at large.

positive value in our society, relationships such as friendship, marriage, and parenthood. Also note that the state of our society is such that the individual appears to have the highest potential to successfully select the recipients of her care, liking, and love (as opposed to such external parties as the state); for example, the individual appears to be the most effective selector of her own friends. Given these points, allocating the individual privacy promotes relationships; for example, extending privacy over decisions about friendships appears to be the most successful way to produce friendships. Assuming that privacy promotes valued relationships, privacy's value might stem from this.[4]

"Personhood" accounts of privacy's value reject the idea that privacy's value stems from its consequences. Instead, they claim that respect for personhood is the foundation of privacy's value. To establish this claim, personhood accounts start with an assumption about what it is to be a person in the moral sense. Stanley Benn explicitly states this assumption: a person is a "subject with a consciousness of himself as an agent, one who is capable of having projects, and assessing his achievements in relation to them."[5] Given this view of personhood, it follows that "to *conceive* someone as a person is to see him as actually or potentially a chooser."[6] In other words, the potential for rational choice is at the core of personhood. Assuming that persons are fundamentally self-determining choosers, we encounter prescriptive requirements concerning individualism. Specifically, it is generally morally desirable to allocate an agent free choice with respect to her preferences. To allow the preferences of others to shape and dictate the agent's actions is to deny the agent's nature as a chooser. This denial can take two forms. First, by dictating the actions of another, an agent might mean to use the other as an instrument of her own ends; this case involves acknowledging that the other is a chooser, but denying her exercise of choice because her choices conflict with the ends of the agent. Second, by dictating the actions of another, an agent might show that she understands the other to be a being incapable of forming and living by their own plans; this case involves denying that the other is a chooser in the first place. To respect a person as a chooser, we must avoid both forms of denial. Assuming that respect for persons entails allowing them the autonomy to be self-determining choosers, this requirement clearly cuts across all realms of the agent's life—not only is there a moral presumption in favor of the agent choosing her own make of car, job, and vacation spot, there is also a presumption in favor of her choosing the objects of her love, liking, and care.[7] As privacy protects the agent's autonomy with respect to her choices about the distribution of her love, liking, and care, the connection between the value of personhood and the value accorded to privacy by the personhood theories is clear: assuming we value respecting persons as rational choosers, we must also value privacy and its protection of a realm of choice for the agent with respect to her love, liking, and care.

Having presented the two possible sources of privacy's value, the promotion of relationships or respect for persons as choosers, the next step is to evaluate these candidates. In what follows, I argue that neither offers a completely satisfactory explanation of privacy's value.

On initial inspection, it seems impossible to deny that we place a positive value on privacy because it promotes the creation and maintenance of close relationships. Consider the assumptions that appear to undergird privacy's protection of decisions concerning intimate activities and actions. First, care, liking, and love cannot be forced. Second, care, liking, and love are intrinsic to truly intimate acts, actions, and activities. Third, intimate acts, actions, and activities are constitutive of close relationships. Fourth, close relationships are part of the human good. From these assumptions it follows that promoting the desired consequence of close relationships requires allocating individuals control over intimate decisions if they are to have close relationships. This consequentialist reading of privacy's value is not merely a possible reading of these assumptions, but appears to be an inevitable reading. If close relationships require that the agent *necessarily* possess a zone of autonomy to realize them, then privacy, by providing and protecting this zone of autonomy, *does* enable these relationships to be realized. The question is, do close relationships necessarily require privacy for their development?

Even if we reject the argument that relationships require privacy *in principle,* there remains a second argument in support of relationship-promotion accounts of privacy's value: linking privacy's value to the relationships it promotes appears to be dictated by the facts. In many cases, it is impossible to deny that privacy *does* promote desirable consequences in the form of close relationships. Consider the protection privacy extends over our choices concerning friends and parenthood. Because of privacy, we possess a protected realm of autonomy with respect to the objects of our liking or love.[8] Given this autonomy, it appears that conditions are such that we can potentially engage in true friendship and parenthood. But what if this zone of privacy were taken away because the state decided it wished to dictate our friends and parental status?[9] A range of negative consequences might result: we might possess an antipathy toward the state-selected "friend" or child, an antipathy deep enough to preclude liking or love. Even if we initially lacked this antipathy, being forced to engage in "friendship" or "parenthood" might lead to the development of such dislike. In short, the very process of being compelled into a "close" relationship initially seems to preclude a true close relationship. Such undesirable consequences are likely because of the limitations of human psychology and the state's inability to make successful choices. On the side of human psychology, being commanded to like someone does not often lead to liking, and being dictated to love does not often produce love. On the side of the state's limitations, it is difficult to imagine the state successfully selecting our friends or parental status. Hence, it is probable that privacy is either necessary for, or provides the optimal path to, the promotion of close relationships in our society. This close conjunction between privacy and the promotion of relationships tempts us to conclude that the value of privacy lies in this relation.

Having sketched two distinct reasons why we might accept a relationship-promotion explanation of privacy's value, is either correct? I will answer this question in reverse, starting with the second argument: the apparent factual tie between privacy and the creation of close relationships makes a relationship-promotion account of privacy's value unavoidable. While it is impossible to deny that privacy often promotes relationships in our society, this fact does not entail that privacy's value stems from this production. These desirable consequences might be nothing more than a side-product of privacy—we might not extend the protection of privacy over intimate decisions in the hope of promoting close relationships, yet protecting these decisions might *still* result in the promotion of relationships. The fact that privacy *does* promote close relationships does not dictate that privacy's value lies exclusively, or even partially, in these consequences.

Although my first argument appears similar to my second, it contains an important difference. The suggestion in my first argument was not that privacy merely *does* promote close relationships, but that the nature of the agent's love, liking, and care are such that close relationships intrinsically require privacy—the agent's emotional endorsement *cannot* be compelled, thus the creation of valued love-, care-, or liking-dependent relationships requires privacy. If we accept this argument, clearly privacy's value is necessarily partially or wholly rooted in its consequences. But this argument is also flawed. Although it *may* be a psychological truth that the agent's love, care, and liking are difficult to compel, there is no reason to suppose that such compulsion is impossible. In fact, people often end up closely tied after such compulsion. Our everyday lives abound in cases in which autonomy-violating compulsion leads to love, liking, or care. Consider a selection of scenarios: a kidnap victim falls in love with her kidnapper; an arranged marriage leads to love between the partners; a woman compelled to have a child loves the child after its birth. These scenarios reveal that privacy-protected autonomy is not necessary for close relationships. If privacy is only contingently, not intrinsically, connected to the nature of the agent's love, care, and liking, my first argument dissolves into my second, falling victim to the same criticisms it encountered.

Having argued that privacy's value *need not* stem from its promotion of close relationships, I now wish to present the stronger argument that privacy's value *does not* stem from this source. There are two positive reasons to reject a relationship-promotion account. Such an account allows the external world to hold privacy hostage, thus overturning our intuitions about the relation between privacy and the external world. Additionally, it fails to explain our intuitions about the necessarily positive value of privacy.

Assume for the moment that the value of privacy *is* a product of its consequences—the close relationships it promotes. Given this assumption, privacy claims require reference to the state of the external world. Specifically, an appeal to an interest in privacy carries weight only if the state of the world is such that privacy *does* indeed promote close relationships. If the world changes so that the agent no longer has to be given privacy in order to promote close relationships, the agent's privacy claims then lack a foundation. To illustrate this, consider the case of friendship. Given the current state of the world, it seems that the individual in our society is in the best position to select her friends; she knows best whom she likes or might like. Thus, as the world is (call this world *A*), allocating the individual agent privacy with respect to friendship would promote friendships in our society. But imagine that the state of the world changes (call the new world *B*). This change could take a wide range of forms: perhaps a drug is discovered that causes us to like others after it is administered; perhaps a computer is developed capable of selecting our friends with a higher degree of accuracy than that possessed by any individual; perhaps the state discovers that forcing people to imitate "for their own good" the behavior characteristic of friendship leads to more friendships than leaving them to their own devices. Whatever the nature of the change, the end result is that privacy no longer serves as the optimal path to the promotion of relationships in world B. Given this change, an agent's privacy claims also undergo a transformation according to the relationship promotion account of privacy's value. Whereas her privacy claim with respect to friendship is justified in world A, it is no longer justified in world B, since privacy is no longer necessary to promote the desired consequences. This example shows how relationship-promotion explanations of privacy's value attach the validity of privacy claims to the state of the external world. Our claim to privacy is always dependent on whether autonomy is necessary to promote the desired end of close relationships.

Attaching the value of privacy to the relationships it promotes also has repercussions for the character of the value accorded privacy. Assuming that its value lies in promotion of close relationships, privacy will be allocated a positive value in a society such as ours, a society such as world A, in which the agent is the most effective creator of relationships. But consider the value of privacy in world B. Its value would be transformed; privacy would abandon its positive value for a negative or neutral value. Relationship-promotion accounts of privacy's value allow it to retain a positive value only so long as it promotes relationships; when this is no longer the case, privacy's value changes.

I believe relationship-promotion accounts of privacy's value fail because they connect the justification for privacy claims and the value of privacy itself to the external world. Consider how these claims are actually put forward and justified. When I make a privacy claim, perhaps one about friendship, I do not first consider the state of the world. I do not ask whether sources in the external world could effectively promote my friendships. If my claim is challenged, information about the state of the external world does not change its validity. Assume that another challenges my privacy claim with respect to my friendship decisions, explaining that a computer has been designed that is capable of matching me with the "perfect" friend. My claim does *not* lose its point (even assuming that I have absolute confidence in this computer's ability to select "friends"). I would still insist that my decisions about friendship deserve privacy. Instead of being forced to enter friendships according to the dictates of the computer, it should be *my* choice whether or not to use the services of the computer. If asked to justify this argument, I might explain that friendship is the sort of pursuit that demands *my* choice, no matter the success of external choosers. This example illustrates the character of a privacy claim. It is a claim that an agent's choice has a prima facie claim to trump considerations of consequences in the external world; it is not a claim that the agent's choice should be considered merely in light of its relationship consequences.[10] Given that relationship-promotion accounts of privacy's value invert this hierarchy, placing consequentialist considerations over considerations of individual choice, we have one reason to reject them.

Relationship-promotion explanations of privacy's value also fail to accord with our intuitions about privacy's consequence-independent value. If its value flows from the relationships it produces, it is clear privacy will be positively valued only in the world where it does indeed promote close relationships. Should we discover that privacy is actually detrimental to the formation of close relationships, we would no longer accord it a positive value. However, this inverts our intuitions about privacy's value. When my world changes from world *A* to world *B,* not only do my privacy claims still make sense, I still accord privacy the same positive value in these worlds; the changed facts do not undermine the value I accord to privacy. In fact, our intuition about its value in this case is the exact opposite to the intuition that the relationship-promotion picture seems to dictate: privacy is valued *just because* it can halt the intrusions of the external world—even if they are "for our own good." If I were faced with the friend-selecting computer, I would not only explain that privacy claims do not collapse when faced with consequentialist relationship considerations, but that I accord value to privacy for exactly that reason, because it allows me to form *my own* plans with respect to friendships. My plans are valuable just because they are my own, not the plans of an external source; even if the external world could effectively promote my friendships, I would still value privacy's protection against such control. As this example reveals, a claim to privacy not only blocks the claims of the external world, it has a positive value *for this very reason.* Since relationship-promotion accounts of privacy's value do not capture this intuition, we have a second reason to set them aside.

Let me gather together the strands of my argument. First of all, the value of privacy is not necessarily located in its consequences—the promotion of close relationships is neither psychologically nor logically dependent on privacy. Second of all, there are two good reasons to reject such a consequentialist location: it fails to account for both our intuition that privacy protects a realm of autonomy for the agent, in which the agent's choice trumps considerations of consequences, and our intuition about privacy's consequence-independent value.[11] Given these points, the value of privacy cannot be seen as a product of the close relationships it promotes. However, this is not to suggest that we can completely abandon the connection between close relationships and the value of privacy. Privacy *does* protect a realm of autonomy with respect to love, liking, and care, a realm in which people can develop close relationships. Furthermore, our intuitions suggest that it is *because* this realm holds the potential for freely chosen intimacy that we value privacy's protection of it. To accord with these intuitions, we must explain how privacy's value can stem from its protection, not its direct promotion, of intimacy.

The above arguments constitute a rejection of relationship-creation or enhancement accounts of privacy's value. There remains a second possibility: the value of privacy may stem from respect for persons. In what follows, I begin by explaining how respect for persons as choosers can generate privacy's value. I contend that a principle of respect for persons as choosers satisfactorily accounts for the sphere of nonconsequentialist autonomy protected by privacy. However, it fails to explain the distinct value we place on choice with respect to *intimate* decisions; it also fails to distinguish between rationality and the expression of loving, caring, and liking. Hence, privacy's value cannot stem from respect for persons *qua* rational choosers.

A principle of respect for persons is generated from an underlying notion of personhood. Because a human possesses certain morally significant traits of personhood, she is entitled to be treated with respect with regard to those traits. These traits have been characterized in a variety of ways (e.g., self-consciousness and moral agency), but the characteristic that has been brought to the forefront of privacy theory is the human capacity for rational choice.[12] Given that an agent possesses that capacity, it follows that she has a justified moral claim to being treated with the respect due to a person. Onora O'Neill points out that there are two moral demands made by a principle of respect for persons: we must not use another as a mere means, and we must treat them as ends in themselves.[13] As Onora O'Neill notes, the positive duty to treat others as ends in themselves entails promoting and sharing "others' ends *without* taking them over."[14] With respect to persons as choosers, this entails that we must neither unduly constrain the choices of others by failing to support those choices nor must we treat them as though they are incapable of developing plans that embody *their own* choices. Since these demands apply to the choices of others with respect to the object(s) of their liking, love, and care—the realm of privacy—we must support these choices without undermining the agent's ability to make them for herself. Furthermore, we must accord a positive value to privacy if we value respecting persons as rational choosers.

The rational chooser account of privacy's value captures what we value about the structure of privacy—we value possessing a realm of autonomy not linked to consequentialist considerations. According to the rational chooser account, privacy's value stems from the fact that it protects a sphere of autonomy for the agent with respect to her choices about the expression of her love, care, and liking, a sphere of choice that is valuable apart from the consequences of the choices. This is correct. As I have argued, privacy is valued because it protects intimate areas of the agent's life, which are understood as areas over which she should possess autonomy independent of the consequences. This is not to suggest that consequentialist considerations will never overturn our privacy claims—clearly they can in serious circumstances. However, such situations will always involve a violation of a justified privacy claim. A consequentialist trade-off will not take place: the consequentialist considerations will not establish that our privacy claims were not justified in the first place. Furthermore, our privacy claims will always be vulnerable to conflict with those of others; in such cases, the conflicting claims may necessitate violating justified privacy claims. Explaining privacy's value in terms of respect for persons as choosers accounts for this sphere of nonconsequentialist autonomy.

However, an account of privacy's value based on respect for persons as choosers does not capture the value we place on the content of privacy distinct from the value we accord to instances of choice with respect to nonintimate matters. If we accept that privacy's value stems from a principle of respect for persons as rational choosers, it appears that we have no foundation on which to distinguish between the value allocated to privacy and that allocated to freedom of choice with respect to nonintimate matters. This is because, as far as rational choice is concerned, an agent's decisions about the distribution of her love, liking, and care are equivalent to her decisions about such nonintimate matters as whether or not to take a particular job, wear a seat belt, or train for a marathon. In short, choice is not indexed to intimacy. Hence if the value of privacy stems strictly from the value placed on free choice, we cannot place special moral weight on the fact that privacy separates a realm of free choice with respect to intimacy—privacy may be conceptually distinct from freedom of choice with respect to nonintimate matters, but not morally distinct. However, this distorts our privacy intuitions. We value privacy not merely because we value choice, but because we value choice *with respect to intimacy*. Consider the value we accord to possessing privacy with respect to the contents of a personal diary. If asked to explain this value, we might initially reply "Well, I value getting to choose who has access to my diary," but if asked to provide further justification, we would not stop there. We might justifiably add, "I value having this choice *because* I value regulating my expression of *intimacy*." As this example shows, appealing to the value of choice alone stops short of capturing the value of privacy; privacy's value stems from the fact that it protects a *special kind* of choice—intimate choice. Since a principle of respect for persons as rational choosers provides us with no grounds to distinguish between the value accorded to intimate and nonintimate choice, it fails to capture the value of privacy.

There is a second reason to reject explanations of privacy's value based on respect for persons as rational choosers. Such explanations make no attempt to distinguish the expression of love, liking, and care from the exercise of rational choice. According to the rational choice accounts, we value autonomy with respect to our love, liking, and care (the autonomy protected by privacy) because we value choice. For example, we value privacy with respect to our diaries because we wish to have control over our expression of care; we value this control because we value autonomy with respect to our rational choices. But how accurate is it to describe our distribution of love, care, and liking as a by-product of rational choice? As far as our everyday intuitions are concerned, it strikes us as peculiar to claim, "I value having control over my expression of love, care, and liking because I value possessing autonomy with respect to my rational choices." It seems inaccurate, or at least incomplete, to lump together rationality and our expression of emotional states. The source of this uneasiness is that these states are not generally understood as a product of rationality. As Onora O'Neill puts it, "intimacy is not a merely cognitive relationship."[15] But understanding privacy's value in terms of respect for rational choosers does not acknowledge this split between intimacy and cognition. Thus, such an account conceals the potential or true differences between emotional states and rationality.[16]

According to rational chooser accounts of personhood, the trait identifying an agent as a person, her capacity for rational choice, requires respect from others. This respect takes many forms, one of which is privacy. This account of privacy's value has a strength—it explains privacy's nonconsequentialist zone of autonomy. However, its weaknesses outweigh this strength. Although respect for an agent as a chooser does create duties to respect the agent's autonomy, this respect does not create a morally distinct zone of autonomy for the intimate decisions protected under privacy. Furthermore, explaining privacy's value in terms of rational choice does not account for our intuition that emotions, such as love, care, and liking, are not equivalent to rationality. Given these difficulties, we must conclude that explaining privacy's value in terms of respect for rational choosers fails to explain the value of privacy as a special, morally distinct realm of autonomy.

We appear to have reached an impasse. On the one hand, relationship-promotion accounts of privacy's value are unsuccessful—they cannot account for the structure of privacy claims. Despite this failure, such accounts capture the fact that privacy is tied to something special about close relationships. On the other hand, rational chooser accounts of privacy's value also fail. If we understand persons as nothing more than choosers, we cannot explain the distinctive value of privacy's content, that is, the distinctive value we accord to control over *intimate* decisions. Yet the zone of autonomy generated by a principle of respect for persons does accord with our privacy intuitions—we *do* value privacy because it provides us with a sphere of autonomy not contingent upon consequentialist considerations. In short, neither of these explanations of privacy's value is satisfactory, yet neither can be altogether abandoned. An escape from this impasse lies in combining the two. I argue that we need to understand persons as autonomous agents with the potential for love, care, and liking—emotional choosers with the potential for relationships. Given this relationship-focused understanding of personhood, the value of privacy can be explained in terms of respect for persons.

There is more to being a person than the capacity for rationality alone. A number of other human capacities are equally distinctive of personhood—specifically, an agent's capacity for liking, loving, and caring.[17] As I have mentioned, such positively valued emotional states as these are not commonly viewed as manifestations of rationality, yet the capacity to experience these states still seems to be intrinsic to personhood. If an agent were rendered incapable of experiencing any of these states, perhaps through extensive psychological trauma, our response to her loss would extend beyond thinking that she had lost some highly desirable, though nonintrinsic, part of her being. We might reasonably wonder about the personhood of the mutilated individual, perhaps questioning whether she could still be held morally accountable for her actions.[18] Similarly, if we encountered someone who had led a life devoid of care, liking, or love, we might exclaim, "But that's no life at all!" In such a situation, our exclamation is clearly not intended to suggest that the individual has lacked biological life, but to suggest that she has lacked a dimension of personhood, that her life has been fundamentally flawed. These scenarios suggest that our notion of personhood requires reference to the human potential for loving, caring, and liking as well as rationality.[19]

If personhood makes claims on the agent as both an emotional and a rational being, it follows that an adequate principle of respect for persons must incorporate respect for each aspect: to respect another as a person is to respect her as both a rational chooser and an emotional chooser, a being with the capacity to make decisions with respect to her love, care, and liking.[20] We must respect the agent's autonomy with regard to loving, caring, and liking as well as rational choice.[21] As for what such respect demands, I see no reason to reject the formulation I mentioned earlier, Onora O'Neill's claim that "there are two separate aspects to treating others as persons: the maxim must not use them (negatively) as mere means, but must also (positively) treat them as ends in themselves."[22] Rather than merely not using others and treating them as ends *qua* rational choosers, I suggest we must *also* not use others and treat them as ends with respect to their status as emotional choosers, as loving, liking, and caring beings.

Let us return to the question of privacy's value. I initially suggested that the value of privacy was based on a principle of respect for persons. Yet, given a traditional principle of respect for persons as rational choosers, the distinctive value of privacy could not be explained. The solution to this quandary is now apparent. A principle of respect for persons as rational choosers *does* support a general principle of respecting an agent's autonomy, since choice presupposes autonomy. But respect for persons also demands reference to another principle. A principle of respect for persons as "emotional choosers" supports a narrower ideal of respecting an agent's autonomy with respect to the choices that embody her love, liking, and care. It is this second aspect of a principle of respect for persons that accounts for the value of privacy. Assuming that society values respecting agents as persons with the capacity to love, care, and like, it follows that society must value protecting the autonomy of these agents with respect to these emotions. To embody this value, society must provide the agents with a zone in which society neither uses them nor fails to treat them as ends in themselves with respect to their intimate lives—the zone of privacy. Because we value respecting persons as autonomous agents with the capacity for love, liking, and care, we value privacy. The question is, how does privacy embody our respect for others as autonomous loving, caring, and liking beings?

By allocating the agent control over intimate decisions, privacy performs two usually overlapping, though conceptually separable, functions. First, it protects the agent's freedom of action. This is most readily apparent in the privacy cases that have been grouped together under constitutional privacy. For example, in *Roe v. Wade* the agent's privacy claim protected her freedom to have an abortion.[23] In *Griswold v. Connecticut,* the agent's privacy claim protected her freedom to use contraceptives.[24] Second, it gives rise to duties of noninterference or nonparticipation in the intimate life of the agent on the part of others. This is most evident in the privacy restrictions concerning access, restrictions commonly embodied in tort privacy law. In privacy cases involving access, the focus is on restricting the access of others to the agent without regard for whether this prohibited access curtails the agent's freedom of action. For example, when an agent makes a privacy claim against the actions of a peeping Tom, her claim is not a claim to curtail the peeping Tom's actions insofar as they curtail her own actions. It is a claim that the peeping Tom should not encroach upon an area of her life even if this encroachment does not interfere with her freedom of action; the peeping Tom could not avoid her privacy claim by arguing that she would never notice him.[25] Given these two aspects of privacy claims—their protection of the agent's freedom of action and the duties of nonintervention they place upon others—how do these aspects protect the agent's autonomy with respect to her expression of care, love, and liking?

It is clear that an agent must be accorded freedom of intimate action if she is to be treated with the respect due to her as an autonomous moral person with the capacity to love, care, and like. A failure to accord the agent this respect via freedom of action can take the form of forbidding, curtailing, or dictating her actions. I cannot be said to respect an agent's autonomy with respect to her love, care, and liking if I forbid her to express or communicate these emotions through action, for example, if I forbid an agent to be a mother, despite the fact that I recognize that motherhood is a vital expression of love for her. Neither do I respect her autonomy with respect to these emotions if I seriously curtail her expression of them in action, for example, if I tell an agent that she is only "free" to be a mother in the setting of a traditional heterosexual family. Finally, I do not respect her autonomy with regard to these emotions if I dictate her actions, for example, if I require an agent to be a mother to fulfill my purposes, fully understanding that mothering is dependent on the agent's love. These points are not surprising, since forbidding, curtailing, and dictating an agent's actions are standard autonomy violations.

It is more difficult to understand the rationale underlying external participation restrictions enforced by privacy—what I will term privacy's "duties of nonintervention." These include such duties as the duty not to read another's diary, the duty not to place a tape recorder in another's bedroom, and the duty not to grab a woman's breast. After all, insofar as the participation of others does not interfere with the agent's freedom of action with respect to her expression of her love, care, and liking, why should this participation violate the respect due to her as an autonomous originator of love, care, and liking? Unlike constraining the agent's action, this failure to acknowledge the other does not consist of an attempt to reduce or regulate her "space" for the expression of love, liking, or care. It consists of a failure to acknowledge what the other's ends are. This failure takes the form of damaging or violating the other's conception of herself as an autonomous source of love, care, and liking.

To be an agent who is capable of entering into close relationships based on care, liking, and love, an agent requires more than the capacity to shape her future actions. Perhaps even more basically, she needs to recognize that she is a person capable of engaging in such relationships, that is, a person capable of freely choosing to express love, liking, and care through her actions. Unfortunately, this recognition is not automatic. It can be damaged when others assume a false position of intimacy with respect to the agent. Joseph Kupfer describes this as damage to the agent's "self-concept":

> When the appearance of intimacy is created through . . . the loss . . . of control over who can experience or know about us, our self-concept is

threatened. By blurring the distinction between intimate and stranger, the pseudo-intimacy seems to force a "false" entry into our self-concept. . . . We feel *as if* we had no choice concerning who our friends really are, as if anyone by *his* choice could make himself our intimate. . . . This sense of threat is sometimes felt when a mere acquaintance slaps us on the shoulder, grins and alludes to a camaraderie not really there.[26]

Alternatively, this damage can be thought of as stripping the meaning of the language of intimacy for the agent, thus undermining her sense that her love, care, and liking are hers to offer, or not offer, to others. Let me illustrate this argument with the example of friendship. The care underlying friendship is commonly expressed by such actions as letting another into your house, allowing her closer physical contact than would be allowed to a stranger, and telling her personal information. These actions receive their importance from the fact that they derive their meaning and value for the agent from her liking for the friend. But given the meaning and value the agent imbues in these actions, actors in the external world can fail to acknowledge this meaning and value. They can wander freely in and out of her room, touch her body as they will, and learn all matters of personal information about her.[27] Given such violations, it is difficult to imagine how the agent involved would ever recognize herself as an originator of friendships. Her liking would not be understood as hers to give (or not to give) to others because society had never acknowledged it as her own. In such a case, others fundamentally fail to respect the agent as a person in the emotional sense since they do not acknowledge that her ends include possessing a self-concept as an autonomous originator of love, care, and liking.

If an agent's autonomy with respect to her love, care, and liking can be damaged when others intrude into her life without acknowledging her as an autonomous source of love, care, and liking (without interfering with her freedom of action), how can this damage be protected against? In order to create and sustain individuals who recognize their capacity for love, liking, and care, the agent needs to be accorded a conventionally defined zone in which others cannot do such things as freely gain access to the agent's body, thoughts, personal information, letters, and so forth—a context for intimacy that generates duties on the part of others not to access the agent. Control over this zone needs to be allocated to the agent without regard for whether she actually needs it in order to prevent others from directly interfering with her intimacy-expressing actions. By according the agent this zone of nonintervention, we convey to her that she is truly an autonomous originator of intimacy, a person who has control over a context, which she is free to imbue with emotional significance. Let me give an example of how this zone works. Consider our privacy-related duty to refrain from sexual contact with another's body without permission, even if this contact would not interfere with their freedom of action. What would happen if we lacked such a duty? If others were free to make sexual contact with an agent at will, the agent would justifiably argue that society was failing to respect and acknowledge, not merely her body, but the body's emotional significance, its connection to the expression of love, liking, and care. Through providing the agent with a conventionally defined zone of nonintervention with respect to sexual contact, we convey to her our acknowledgement of the significance of sexual behavioral markers of intimacy and, hence, the emotions that find expression in them. By providing the agent with control over these behavioral markers, we convey to her that she is free to offer, or not to offer, her love to others through sexual contact.[28] Hence, she comes to understand herself as a potential originator of intimacy because she understands herself to have control over the behavioral language that expresses intimacy.

Let me summarize my argument up to this point. To be respected as a person with the capacity for love, care, and liking, an agent needs a zone with two characteristics: a zone in which she possesses autonomy of action and a zone that gives rise to duties of noninterference from external parties. To satisfy the first requirement, the agent requires autonomy with respect to the actions she takes to embody her love, liking, and care; society must not use the agent in such a way that she lacks the autonomy of action to express these emotions. To satisfy the second requirement, the agent requires a zone to which she can regulate the access of others (including informational access); society must not use the agent in such a way that she is rendered incapable of understanding herself as a source of intimacy. Providing her with such a zone enables her to develop and sustain a self-concept as an originator of love, liking, and care. However, these two arguments are only sufficient to create a contingent sphere of autonomy with respect to intimacy, that is, privacy, for the agent. These arguments only establish that respecting an agent as a person with the capacity for love, liking, and care entails not blocking her route to intimacy; they say nothing about why we should necessarily respect the agent's own choices with respect to intimacy. This leaves us with a paternalistic challenge: if we truly believe that the expression of love, liking, and care are essential to personhood, then it would seem that we would have an obligation to interfere with the agent's freedom of action when we could protect her access to stable close relationships by such interference. Similarly, we should restrict an agent's zone of nonintervention if such restriction were necessary to protect her access to intimacy, assuming that we could do so in a sufficiently subtle way so as to not diminish her capacity for close relationships. After all, if we allow an agent autonomy to protect her access to intimacy, why should we refrain from limiting her autonomy if this limitation were necessary to protect her access to intimacy?

To answer this question, recall that I have been arguing that we must respect others not merely as emotional beings, but as emotional *choosers*. As I have discussed, to respect people as emotional choosers, we must not only allow them to lead lives in which they are capable of expressing love, liking, and care, we must also allow them choice with respect to such lives. In other words, we must not only avoid using people in such a way as to preclude intimacy, we must also treat them as ends in themselves with respect to their intimate lives. To do this requires acknowledging others as capable of forming their *own* plans with respect to intimacy and its constitutive close relationships, plans we respect by not taking them over. This suggests that it is not enough for an agent to have freedom of action once she has entered into close relationships; prior to such freedom she must have the freedom to decide whether she indeed wishes to enter into relationships based on care, liking, and love and how she wishes to create these relationships. She must have control over her own construction of intimacy, without regards for whether her plans best protect her access to intimacy. This requires not only allowing her to freely create her own relationships, but also allowing her to refuse close relationships. To illustrate this point, consider forcing a woman to have a child. Our respect for a woman as an emotional chooser would preclude forcing her into having a child, even if we were aware that she planned to do so in the near future and we were convinced that such compulsion would promote real intimacy. Such compulsion would reveal that we failed to respect the woman's claim to plan her own intimate life, perhaps that we did not even think her capable of creating such plans. Such free relationship creation, or refusal of creation, cannot take place unless the agent is allowed to make her own decisions about her intimate, relationship-building acts and activities, decisions that cover both matters involving her actions and nonintervention from the external world. We now have a reply to the paternalist's challenge: paternalistic interference with an agent's decisions might indeed protect her access to intimacy, but far more is at stake here than being able to express love, liking, and care. We value being respected as autonomous emotional agents who can form their own life plans with respect to intimacy. Hence, privacy protects us from both manipulative and paternalistic intervention into our zone of autonomy with respect to intimacy.

So, we now see that respecting someone as an emotional chooser with respect to love, liking, and care requires granting them various forms of freedom: the freedom of action necessary to express intimacy, freedom to create themselves as an originator of intimacy, and freedom of choice with respect to intimacy. Combining these requirements, it is clear that respecting another as an emotional chooser with respect to love, liking, and care demands that we accord them privacy. This emotional chooser account of privacy's value reveals that the positive value we accord to privacy in our liberal society is not tied to the consequences it promotes, close relationships, nor to a narrow principle of respect for rational choosers. Privacy's positive value stems from a principle of respect for persons as autonomous beings with the capacity for love, care, and liking, beings with an invaluable capacity for freely chosen close relationships; this principle dictates the positive value we accord to the agent's control over intimate decisions about her own actions and her decisions about intimate access to herself. Without this underlying notion of persons as emotional choosers, we would not recognize that the agent's sphere of autonomy with respect to her care, liking, and love is a sphere over which she has evident moral rulership, a rulership that deserves the respect and protection of society. In the next chapter, I discuss how privacy law acknowledges and protects the value we accord to the agent's zone of autonomy with respect to intimacy, her zone of privacy.

Notes

1. Despite the cumbersome nature of defining intimacy in terms of the agent's love, care, or liking, this repeated usage in this chapter is necessary to capture the range of emotions protected by privacy.

2. It may seem as though I have already explained the value of privacy. After all, in Chapter 4 I argued that privacy is a presumptive moral good: we accord it a necessarily positive value. Though I assume privacy's positive value in what follows, I still need to explain why we attribute this value to privacy.

3. It may appear that I am contradicting myself. In my introduction, I limited my project to explaining privacy's value in a liberal Western context, yet now I claim that privacy's value stems from a theory of personhood, a seemingly universal category. However, this is only an apparent contradiction: personhood accounts of privacy's value invoke liberal Western accounts of personhood.

4. Examples of relationship-creation accounts of privacy's value include Charles Fried, "Privacy," *Yale Law Journal* 77 (1968): 475–93; Robert Gerstein, "Intimacy and Privacy," *Ethics* 89 (1978): 86–91; James Rachels, "Why Privacy is Important," *Philosophy and Public Affairs* 4 (1975): 323–33. Note that these philosophers account for the value of privacy defined differently than it is in this work; hence, their arguments do not always apply.

5. Stanley Benn, "Privacy, Freedom, and Respect for Persons," in *Privacy: Nomos XIII,* ed. J. Roland Pennock and John W. Chapman (New York: Atherton Press, 1971), 8–9.

6. Benn, "Privacy, Freedom, and Respect for Persons," 8–9.

7. Clearly this presumption is merely that—a presumption. Given opposing claims, it may be violated without doing moral harm to the agent.

8. As I have noted, I do not provide a precise characterization of the agent's emotional stance. For the purposes of my argument, all that must be accepted is that relationships such as friendship and parenthood require some combination of love, care, and liking.

9. Though I assume here that the state violates our privacy, this assumption is not essential; another privacy violator could be assumed.

10. Of course, prima facie privacy claims are not immune to conflict, including conflict generated by consequentialist considerations. An agent's privacy claims are always vulnerable to conflict with the moral claims of others; in such cases, the conflicting claims may necessitate a justified violation of one set of claims. In certain serious circumstances, consequentialist moral claims might lead to a violation of autonomy-based privacy claims.

11. These two reasons to reject a relationship-creation account of privacy's value are not altogether distinct—privacy is accorded a positive value because it protects a realm of individual autonomy.

12. See Benn, "Privacy, Freedom, and Respect for Persons."

13. Onora O'Neill, "Between Consenting Adults," *Philosophy and Public Affairs* 14 (1985): 262.

14. O'Neill, "Between Consenting Adults," 265.

15. O'Neill, "Between Consenting Adults," 270.

16. I do not mean to deny that intimacy is an emotional state that only rational

beings may experience. I accept that the human capacity for love, care, and liking might be incorporated into a broad conception of rationality. However, I find no indication that such a broad view of rationality underlies the work of such rational chooser privacy theorists as Stanley Benn.

17. I do not mean to suggest that these emotional states are the only emotional states essential to personhood, only that they are at least *among* this group.

18. For example, we might not hold her morally responsible for failing to visit a dying friend.

19. This discussion of personhood requires far more development than I can provide here. All I hope to have pointed out is that personhood has both a rational and emotional aspect.

20. I am not attempting to put forward any thesis about the relation between emotionality and rationality. I am suggesting that *if* we accept the traditional view that the capacity for emotion and rationality are distinct categories (if not antithetical ones), our notion of moral personhood still requires reference to both of these categories. If we saw emotions as an outgrowth of rationality, a principle of respect for persons as rational beings would entail the same conclusions.

21. At this point, my ideas parallel those of John Stuart Mill: ''To a certain extent it is admitted that our understanding should be our own; but there is not the same willingness to admit that our desires and impulses should be our own likewise. . . . Yet desires and impulses are as much part of a perfect human being as beliefs and restraints.'' See John Stuart Mill, *On Liberty* (Indianapolis: Hackett Publishing Co., 1978), 57.

22. O'Neill, ''Between Consenting Adults,'' 262.

23. Roe v. Wade, 410 U.S. 113 (1973).

24. Griswold v. Connecticut, 381 U.S. 479 (1965).

25. I do not intend this division between constitutional privacy cases as involving concerns about the agent's freedom of action and tort privacy cases as involving concerns about the interference of others in the agent's private sphere to be anything more than a heuristic device. Depending on the reading we bring to constitutional and tort privacy cases, they can often be assimilated into either camp. For example, *Roe v. Wade* can be read as being concerned with the government's participation in the intimate life of the individual, not her freedom of action. Additionally, I do not intend to suggest that the categories of individual freedom of action and external participation in the agent's life (the case of the peeping Tom) are antithetical—they are not.

26. Joseph Kupfer, ''Privacy, Autonomy, and Self-Concept,'' *American Philosophical Quarterly* 24 (1987): 86.

27. Assume that she is still free to do such things as allow others into her home as a sign of liking, allow another to touch her body as a sign of love, and to reveal personal information to those she cares for. Hence, the damage to her privacy does not lie in damage done to her freedom of action.

28. Since society must construct this nonintervention zone in terms of broad, socially defined behavioral markers of intimacy, it has to act indirectly, according people control over intimate access whether or not intimacy is actually at stake with respect to a particular instance of access. For example, society provides the agent with control over who sees her undressed, thus acknowledging the emotional significance that can be attached to such a display. However, this entails that the agent will also be able to determine who sees her undressed in the bathroom, even if such a display has little to do with conveying emotion. Similarly, society's duty not to access the bedrooms of its citizens will hold whether or not individual citizens are actually using their bedrooms for intimate purposes.

8

Intimacy-Based Privacy: The Answer to Legal Privacy Debates

According to a possibly apocryphal story, in 1883 the tabloid presses began to run lurid stories about the home life of Samuel Warren. Dismayed at being the center of public attention, Warren discussed the situation with his legal colleague Louis Brandeis. Warren and Brandeis then staged a legal counterattack against yellow journalism. In their article, "The Right to Privacy," they argued that the intimacies of the "domestic circle" merited the protection of privacy, despite the fact that claims to privacy lacked legal precedent.[1] With this article, Warren and Brandeis established the foundation of tort privacy law.

In 1961, Estelle Griswold committed a crime, fully realizing that she would be charged with it. As the director of the Connecticut Planned Parenthood League, she distributed information about the use of contraceptives to married couples. This act violated a Connecticut law prohibiting either the use of contraceptives or the distribution of information concerning their use. When she was charged with this crime, she immediately confessed to it, since she sought to have it tried as a test case for Connecticut's law. She was promptly fined by the Connecticut court. Instead of paying this fine, she appealed the ruling to the Supreme Court, arguing that the Connecticut law infringed upon her constitutionally protected right to privacy. After considering her case, the Court issued a landmark ruling. It ruled that Connecticut's law unconstitutionally infringed upon a fundamental right to privacy inhering in the marital relationship. *Griswold v. Connecticut* was the first case to identify an independent constitutional right to privacy.[2]

Although the concerns of Samuel Warren, Louis Brandeis, and Estelle Griswold have long since been resolved, tort and constitutional privacy law continue to thrive. Both areas of law have expanded far beyond the concerns originally voiced by Warren, Brandeis, and Griswold, protecting areas of life that seem remote from yellow journalism and contraceptives. The tort of privacy has been cited in cases involving the appropriation or public disclosure of information about an individual and intrusion upon an individual.[3] The constitutional right to privacy has been cited in rulings involving matters as diverse as child rearing, the home, and abortion.[4] Despite, or perhaps because of, the rapid growth of privacy law, the right to privacy has been, and continues to be, widely criticized as "pernicious" and "a malformation of constitutional law."[5] Critics of both tort and constitutional privacy law contend that neither area of law possesses a conceptual focus. Furthermore, they argue that neither area of law protects a distinct moral interest. Finally, they suggest that tort and constitutional privacy law lack a shared theoretical foundation. Assuming my definition of privacy and account of its value, I wish to respond to these criticisms.[6] According to my account, intimacy is the feature that links together the bulk of tort and constitutional privacy law. Furthermore, a focus on intimacy allows us to see how tort and constitutional privacy are internally unified—since our interest in intimacy is conceptually and morally separable from nonprivacy interests, it provides a conceptual and moral core for much of tort and constitutional privacy. Finally, and perhaps most importantly, an intimacy-based account of privacy allows us to critique certain truly pernicious developments in both tort and constitutional privacy law.

As I have mentioned, the constitutional right to privacy protects claims to autonomy with respect to decisions about such matters as child rearing, family relationships, procreation, marriage, and the home. Constitutional privacy criticism develops along two lines. One line focuses on the contention that the right to privacy conflicts with various standards of constitutional interpretation; for example, the right to privacy is argued not to be inferable from the "original intent" of the writers of the Constitution. Hence, the right to privacy is claimed to be constitutionally invalid. Although this criticism of the constitutional foundation for the right to privacy is philosophically interesting, it is not considered further in this work; a second line of anticonstitutional privacy criticism is explored. Instead of focusing on arguments that the right to privacy conflicts with its external constitutional framework, this second line of criticism focuses on the claim that the constitutional right to privacy is internally flawed. In the useful words of Ferdinand Schoeman, the right to privacy is said to be neither coherent nor distinct.[7] In this section, I consider two arguments that are made to support this claim. The first of these is that the right to privacy is internally malformed because it lacks coherence, that is, there is no common denominator linking the interests protected by constitutional privacy.[8] The second argument is that the right to privacy is malformed because it is not morally distinct, in other words, the right to privacy can be "dissolved" into another right, specifically the right to liberty or autonomy, without moral loss.[9] In what follows, I argue that constitutional privacy law can avoid each of these criticisms: the emerging constitutional right to privacy is both conceptually and morally focused due to its dependence on intimacy. However, as I will show, the Court's ruling in the case of *Bowers v. Hardwick* threatens this focus.[10]

The first criticism of the constitutional right to privacy is that it lacks coherence, protecting merely an arbitrary assortment of interests. It is easy to see what underlies this charge. We need only scan some of the cases decided on the grounds of constitutional privacy, noting how they seem to involve totally unrelated interests. For example, consider the group of cases consisting of *Stanley v. Georgia, Loving v. Virginia,* and *Roe v. Wade.*[11] In *Stanley v. Georgia,* the plaintiff argued that Georgia's law prohibiting his possession of illegal obscene materials in his home violated his constitutional right to privacy; the Court agreed with his argument. In *Loving v. Virginia,* the plaintiffs contended that Virginia's law prohibiting interracial marriages violated their right to privacy; the Court accepted this argument. Finally, in *Roe v. Wade,* the plaintiff argued that a Texas law prohibiting abortions violated her right to privacy; once again, the Court accepted this argument. On initial inspection, it certainly appears as though these cases are concerned with radically different matters: pornography, interracial marriage, and abortion. The impression of arbitrariness generated by this small selection of cases is only heightened when we consider the range of interests that the Supreme Court has declared privacy protected, focusing on such matters as child rearing, family relationships, procreation, marriage, the home, contraception, and abortion. In this list, we find interests concerning the individual and those focusing on the group, interests focusing on property and those involving the body, interests concerning having children and those focusing on *not* having children. A common denominator does not immediately emerge. Lacking this, it is simple to interpret the diversity of interests protected by privacy as mere incoherence, leading to the conclusion that the right to privacy is itself incoherent. We must stop short of this.

Reconsider the areas protected under the constitutional right to privacy: child rearing, family relationships, procreation, marriage, the home, contraception, and abortion. These areas of life are dissimilar under *certain* descriptions; for example, if I describe the privacy-protected realm of the home in terms of property, family relationships in terms of claims to personal relations, and abortion in terms of claims not to bear children, it may indeed be impossible to locate a similarity that justifies including all of these areas within the scope of the right to privacy. However, given my characterization of privacy as protecting the agent's autonomy with respect to intimacy, we are led to wonder whether these apparently disparate areas might be gathered together under the common heading of intimacy.

A close reading of a variety of constitutional privacy cases reveals that the Court explicitly and implicitly appeals to a common intimacy-based description across its privacy rulings. Consider some of the previously discussed privacy cases. In *Griswold v. Connecticut,* the right to privacy was held to be involved because Connecticut's anticontraceptive law curtailed the "intimate marital relation."[12] Connecticut's law infringed upon it because restricting access to contraceptives clearly limited the married couple's autonomy to express affection through sexual interaction. In *Stanley v. Georgia,* Georgia's law prohibiting the ownership of obscene materials at home was described as a privacy issue because it concerned the *privacy of the home,* the home being seen as a sanctuary for intimacy.[13] Georgia's law undermined the intimacy of the home because it failed to acknowledge the home's status as a place where close emotional ties are forged. In *Roe v. Wade,* Texas's law prohibiting abortion was understood as involving privacy concerns because it involved a woman's "intimate personal decision,"[14] infringing upon it by restricting access to abortion, which not only limits women's autonomy with respect to the sexual expression of affection but curtails their freedom with respect to the emotional ties of motherhood. More generally, the Court has stated that the right to privacy protects a realm of decisions about "personal intimacies,"[15] that is, acts that embody love, care, and liking. The point of these examples is that the Court is not proceeding in a merely *ad hoc* fashion in delineating the right to privacy, that it is *not* working with descriptions of privacy-protected relationships, spatial areas, and areas of the body that cast these into unrelated sets—the Court is working with descriptions that treat these areas of life as *subsets* of the central set of intimacy.

My argument that the common denominator of constitutional privacy is intimacy merely establishes that the right to privacy is coherent. There remains a second criticism—that the constitutional right to privacy lacks moral distinctness. According to this, the moral significance of privacy claims can be explained *without* resorting to an independent right to privacy; we need only appeal to the right to liberty to fully understand the wrong involved in constitutional privacy violations.[16] The argument has two steps. The first is taken by both critics and defenders of constitutional privacy; they observe that constitutional privacy delineates a realm of liberty or autonomy for the agent. For example, privacy critic Hyman Gross says that "in the *Griswold* situation there had been an attempt by government to regulate personal affairs . . . so there was an issue regarding autonomy."[17] David Richards, a defender of constitutional privacy, agrees with Gross; he notes that the constitutional right to privacy "turns on some form of substantive liberty or autonomy to act in certain ways without threat of sanction."[18] Having taken this initial step, critics diverge from defenders and introduce prescriptive claims in their next step.[19] They argue that, since constitutional privacy claims are liberty claims, the value we accord to privacy is simply the value we accord to liberty from state regulation; hence we should abandon talk about the value accorded to privacy, focusing instead on that accorded to liberty.

Constitutional privacy claims *are* a species of liberty claims. A claim to constitutional privacy is a claim to possess autonomy with respect to an intimate area of life. This fact is readily illustrated by a brief survey of constitutional privacy cases. *Griswold v. Connecticut* protects the liberty of the married couple with respect to "marital intimacies." Similarly, *Roe v. Wade* protects the liberty of women to have abortions, while *Stanley v. Georgia* protects our liberty from undue state intervention in the home. But acknowledging that the constitutional right to privacy protects a realm of liberty does not entail that the value accorded to privacy is indistinguishable from the value accorded to liberty from undue state regulation. As I have mentioned in my discussion of Judith

Jarvis Thomson's reductionist argument, if we jump from the assumption that privacy rights are a subset of rights to liberty to the conclusion that there is no need to discuss the value of the right to privacy, we neglect the fact that even a subset can have a significance that is not reducible to the significance of the set from which it was derived. Although privacy protects a realm of liberty, we may place a distinct value on protecting this realm, a value predicated on the value of intimacy.

Setting aside the bare bones of logical possibility, what evidence do I have that moral justifications for constitutional privacy claims do not, in reality, collapse into appeals to the value of liberty from state interference? The initial evidence is empirical: constitutional privacy claims are morally distinct from liberty claims since privacy claims are extended more stringent legal protection than are liberty claims. To understand this, we must distinguish between the right to privacy's status as a "fundamental right" and the right to liberty's lack of such status. On the one hand, the privacy cases that have developed in the wake of *Griswold* make it explicitly clear that privacy is a so-called fundamental constitutional right. As Justice Blackmun explains in the case of *Roe v. Wade,* "only personal rights that can be deemed 'fundamental' . . . are included in [the constitutional] guarantee of personal privacy."[20] On the other hand, as Justice Rehnquist notes in his dissenting opinion to *Roe v. Wade,* there is no fundamental constitutional right to liberty.[21] Rather, there is the Fourteenth Amendment's provision that no state may "deprive any person of life, liberty, or property, without due process of law." This distinction between "fundamental" and nonfundamental constitutional rights may initially appear to be nothing more than legal quibbling, but this impression is misleading; the distinction has important legal ramifications. As Judith DeCew notes, "current constitutional standards . . . require 'strict scrutiny' for cases concerning 'fundamental values' and privacy has been judged to be one such value. Thus . . . privacy claims have a greater chance of being protected when they conflict with other rights or general interests than they would have if only liberty, or freedom from governmental interference, were involved.[22] In other words, within the confines of constitutional law, the domain of privacy is *not* treated as morally equivalent to the domain of liberty. The right to privacy—that is, the right to autonomy with respect to intimacy—is treated as morally distinct in that it is *more* morally stringent than the class of liberty claims as a whole.

Of course, demonstrating that the constitutional right to privacy *is* accorded more stringent legal protection than the right to liberty does not prove that constitutional privacy *ought to be* accorded this protection. The Court might be making a mistake in according the right to privacy the privileged status of a fundamental right. In attempting to establish its moral distinctness, the Court might have observed that the right to privacy is conceptually distinct from the right to liberty, and then leaped to the conclusion that the right to privacy is morally distinct. Unfortunately, there is not enough momentum to support this leap. While the constitutional right to privacy *is* conceptually distinct from the right to liberty—privacy protects a zone of autonomy with respect to intimacy, whereas the sphere of liberty is not indexed to intimacy—conceptual distinctions do not necessarily carry moral weight. For example, if I were to distinguish a subset of liberty claims concerning green objects from the set of liberty claims as a whole, I would then have a conceptually distinct subset. However, it is implausible to suggest that my "green object" liberty claims would allude to a distinct moral value; the property of greenness is not a property we accord moral significance. In the case of the right to privacy, what needs to be established is that intimacy is a morally relevant property within the domain of constitutional law, a property that distinguishes between the moral weight accorded to privacy claims and that accorded to liberty claims. In other words, it needs to be shown that constitutional privacy is accorded the status of a fundamental right because the Court is according a greater value to the protection of liberty with respect to intimacy than it accords to liberty as a whole.

Intimacy is not merely the conceptually distinguishing feature of constitutional privacy claims—intimacy is also their morally relevant feature. According to constitutional law, it is *because* certain areas of life are intimate and, hence, valued that the agent is provided privacy with respect to them. Similarly, the moral wrong involved in violating constitutionally protected privacy lies in the fact that such violations impinge upon an agent's zone of emotional intimacy, not in the fact that such violations curtail an agent's liberty as a whole. To illustrate these points, consider some of the privacy cases I have discussed previously—*Griswold v. Connecticut, Stanley v. Georgia,* and *Roe v. Wade.*

In *Griswold v. Connecticut,* the Court argued that it is wrong to violate the privacy of the marital relation through anticontraceptive laws. But this wrong was not attributed to the mere fact that the married couple's liberty from undue state regulation was curtailed (though it clearly was). Rather, the Court argued that the marital relation merits privacy *because of its intimacy.* As the Court put it, marriage merits privacy because it "is a coming together for better or for worse . . . intimate to the degree of being sacred."[23] Because the Court understood marriage as intimate, as fundamentally dependent on the partner's love for each other, it ruled that individuals should have control over decisions about the activities constitutive of marriage, including sexual expression. *Griswold* reveals that the Court places a distinct value on privacy, a value predicated on the respect due to persons as emotional agents.

Similarly, in *Stanley v. Georgia,* the Court held that it is wrong to violate another's privacy by restricting her from possessing obscene material at home. The core of this wrong was not attributed to the fact that such a restriction curtails an agent's liberty to watch obscene material as she pleases. In fact, the Court held in *Paris Adult Theatre I v. Slaton* that privacy did not protect the liberty to view obscene materials in commercial theaters.[24] In *Stanley,* the wrong was located in the fact that such restrictions threaten the home, the home being understood as a sanctuary for intimacy.[25] In recognizing the intimacy of the home, the Court acknowledged that an agent merits autonomy with respect to her home due to its significance as a place where close emotional ties are constructed, not merely because it is her property. Thus, the gravamen of *Stanley's* argument focused on the wrong done to an individual by failing to respect her autonomy with respect to an intimate spatial realm; the gravamen did not lie in the harm done to another by simply curtailing her liberty of action in general.

Finally, the Court held in *Roe v. Wade* that a woman's privacy interests protect her access to abortion. Despite the prevalence of the claim that abortion rights stem from women's right to control their own bodies, the Court's argument in *Roe* did not rest on claims about bodily ownership. In fact, the Court has explicitly distanced itself from the idea that restricting a woman's choice concerning abortion is wrong only because it interferes with her liberty to do with her body what she wishes without state regulation.[26] The wrong was attributed to the intimate nature of the liberty being restricted; as Justice Stewart explained, quoting the words of Justice Brennan in *Eisenstadt v. Baird,* restrictions on abortion are wrong because they are an "unwarranted governmental intrusion into matters so fundamentally affecting a person as the decision whether to bear or beget a child."[27] Stewart's quote reveals a twofold moral foundation for abortion access claims. First of all, since a decision about *begetting* a child is intimate—it involves a choice about the emotional ties women wish to construct with their partners—women have a claim to autonomy with respect to this decision. Second of all, since a decision about *bearing* a child is intimate—it involves a choice about whether a woman wishes to enter into a loving relationship with a child—she has a further claim to autonomy. *Roe* demonstrates that privacy is valuable for women because it acknowledges their autonomy with respect to love, liking, and care, not merely their autonomy as physical bodies.[28]

The value accorded to autonomy with respect to intimacy in these specific cases is also evident in the Court's general rationale supporting constitutional privacy decisions. The Court has explained that privacy ought to be protected because we value agents being able to express their "beliefs, their thoughts, [and] their emotions"[29] when these are constitutive of "protected intimate relationships."[30] Because we value agents being able to freely construct intimate relationships, relationships based on care, liking, and love, we accord a positive value to constitutional privacy's protection of intimacy.

Let me summarize my arguments about the moral distinctness of the constitutional right to privacy. Intimacy is not treated as a morally neutral consideration in the Court's privacy rulings; it is understood as the fundamental human interest at stake, meriting more stringent legal protection than is accorded to liberty from state intervention. According to the Court's rationale, we seek to protect privacy because we value intimacy; we condemn the violation of privacy because it violates intimacy. The Court's treatment of privacy cases clearly drives a wedge between the moral value of liberty as a whole and that of privacy. As far as constitutional privacy is concerned, we value privacy-protected liberty because it allows us both literal and figurative room for intimacy; however, clearly we do not value all forms of liberty from state regulation due to reasons of intimacy. Thus, we can distinguish between the value accorded to constitutional privacy and that accorded to liberty from undue state interference.

At this point, my argument is open to an apparently decisive criticism: I have managed to establish that constitutional privacy protects a valued realm of intimacy only by ignoring a constitutional case that vitiates my argument. In 1986, the Supreme Court heard the case of *Bowers v. Hardwick*.[31] In this case, Michael Hardwick challenged the constitutionality of a Georgia statute criminalizing sodomy between consenting adults. Hardwick argued that Georgia's statute violated his constitutional right to privacy. However, the Court rejected Hardwick's argument.

Refusing to address the issue of heterosexual sodomy, the Court ruled that homosexual sexual activity between consenting adults is not protected by the constitutional right to privacy.[32] Yet consenting sexuality is the paradigm of intimacy—sexuality derives its meaning and value for us from its ties to our love, liking, and care. This tension between the Court's ruling and the intimate nature of decisions about consenting sexuality seems to present a significant difficulty for my argument: assuming that decisions about sexuality are intimate, then the Court's refusal to extend the protection of privacy over homosexual sexuality would appear to make it clear that intimacy is not the conceptual and moral core of constitutional privacy.

Although *Bowers* appears to undermine my argument, closer examination shows that it actually strengthens it. In *Bowers,* the Court managed to separate homosexual sexuality from the protection of privacy only by blinding itself to the connection between such sexuality and love, liking, and care. Rather than attempting to link the issues at stake in *Bowers* to past precedent, the Court's majority ruling insisted upon the dissimilarity between homosexual sexuality and the issues previously protected by constitutional privacy: "we think it evident that none of the rights announced in those [previous privacy] cases bears any resemblance to the claimed constitutional right of homosexuals to engage in acts of sodomy. . . . No connection between family, marriage, or procreation on the one hand and homosexual activity on the other has been demonstrated."[33] Despite the Court majority's failure to find this connection, the thread that unites the family, marriage, procreation, and homosexual sexual activity is clear: all of these matters fall within the purview of intimacy and, hence, privacy. Justice Blackmun's dissenting opinion in *Bowers* acknowledges the majority's failure to recognize the intimacy of decisions concerning sexuality: "the Court claims that its decision today merely refuses to recognize a fundamental right to engage in homosexual sodomy; what the Court really has refused to recognize is the fundamental interest all individuals have in controlling the nature of their intimate associations."[34] Due to the Court's failure to locate intimacy as the conceptual and moral core of privacy, the Court was unable to understand the privacy issue at stake in *Bowers.*[35] My intimacy-based account of privacy reveals that the Court has unjustifiably stepped away from its emerging doctrine of privacy in this case—only by ignoring the value it itself had placed upon autonomy with respect to intimacy was the Court able to support *Bowers.* Faced with a clear connection between homosexual activity and past privacy rulings, the Court must reconsider its biased exclusion of homosexual activity from the scope of constitutional privacy if it wishes to retain the protection constitutional privacy extends over the family, marriage, and procreation.

My discussion of constitutional privacy began by introducing two accusations raised against constitutional privacy claims. On the one hand, constitutional privacy was said to lack coherence, consisting of only a heterogenous collection of interests. On the other hand, constitutional privacy was claimed to lack moral distinctness due to the apparent homogeneity of the values protected by privacy and liberty from undue state interference. My response to these criticisms is now clear. Constitutional privacy claims cohere around the notion of intimacy. Given that these claims are a species of liberty claims, they *can* be treated as such. However, such a move only distracts us from the source of the distinct moral value of privacy—its connection to intimacy. Intimacy not only unifies past constitutional privacy issues, it also allows us to criticize the Court's failures to consistently identify and protect the sphere of constitutional privacy.

Setting aside constitutional privacy law for the moment, let us consider the tort of privacy. Tort privacy law is designed to protect agents' claims to have physical and informational access to themselves restricted; it is concerned with the damage individuals can sustain due to unwanted access from others. Due to the existence of tort privacy law, we can seek legal redress against such actions as another intruding into our seclusion, someone disclosing personal facts about our lives, and someone taking embarrassing photographs of our behavior. Despite the large number of cases that have been decided on the ground of tort privacy law since the days of Warren and Brandeis, it is often claimed to suffer from the same flaws as constitutional privacy law: critics contend that the tort of privacy is neither coherent nor morally distinct.[36] These criticisms are outlined in what follows. I suggest that understanding tort privacy as protecting the value we accord to regulating intimate physical and informational access largely undermines these criticisms.[37] Additionally, an intimacy-based account of privacy allows us to criticize certain developments in tort privacy law, specifically the inclusion of property issues within the scope of the tort.

The first criticism of tort privacy law is that it lacks coherence, protecting an unrelated assortment of interests. As William Prosser has argued, an examination of tort privacy cases apparently reveals a wide and disparate range of interests. According to Prosser's well-known categorization, the seemingly unitary tort of privacy should be separated into four distinct torts: "1. Intrusion upon the plaintiff's seclusion or solitude, or into his private affairs. 2. Public disclosure of embarrassing private facts about the plaintiff. 3. Publicity which places the plaintiff in a false light in the public eye. 4. Appropriation, for the defendant's advantage, of the plaintiff's name or likeness."[38] Let me term Prosser's first category the "intrusion" tort, the second two categories the "reputation" tort, and the final category the "appropriation" tort. (By calling these categories "torts," I only mean to suggest that Prosser believes they should be torts.) For Prosser, there is no common denominator that links our claims about seclusion, our name or image, private facts, and the dissemination of disinformation about our lives. To further illustrate the apparent heterogeneity of tort privacy law, consider an assortment of classic legal cases that embody some of Prosser's categories: *De May v. Roberts, Melvin v. Reid,* and *Pavesich v. New England Life Insurance Company.*[39] In *De May,* the plaintiff argued that her privacy was violated by a spectator who watched the plaintiff give birth in her own home. The Michigan court accepted her argument. In *Melvin,* the plaintiff contended that her privacy was violated by a movie that depicted her past life as a prostitute and used her maiden name; the California court agreed. In *Pavesich,* the plaintiff argued that his privacy was violated when his photograph was used to sell life insurance; the Georgia court ruled in his favor. It certainly appears as though these cases are concerned with unrelated matters: the security and seclusion of the home; the urge to conceal embarrassing facts about the past; someone's property interests with respect to her photographic image. Given the apparent lack of a conceptual tie linking these matters, it is not immediately clear why we should group them together under the umbrella of tort privacy law. But should we follow Prosser's lead in only focusing on the diversity of the matters grouped under tort privacy? I think not. After close examination, Prosser's first three privacy categories, which focus on issues concerning intrusion and personal reputation, prove to be both coherent and distinct. Let us consider these issues of intrusion and reputation, setting aside Prosser's fourth tort division for the moment.

As was the case with constitutional privacy, the areas of life grouped under Prosser's intrusion and reputation categories are dissimilar under *certain* descriptions. If we accept Prosser's description of tort privacy matters in terms of seclusion and embarrassing facts about the past, such disparate descriptions will rapidly render tort privacy law incoherent; it is unlikely that we will identify a similarity that will justify including these claims under the scope of privacy. However, if we understand privacy in terms of intimacy, we can locate a common theme in much of tort privacy law that excludes Prosser's disparate descriptions. Consider some of the tort privacy cases I have previously mentioned. In *De May,* the right to privacy was not held to be involved simply because the defendant destroyed the plaintiff's seclusion. Privacy was an issue because the defendant gained *intimate access* to the plaintiff; the defendant entered the realm of the home to witness the "sacred" event of childbirth.[40] As Edward Bloustein puts it, *De May* was upheld on the grounds of privacy because the defendant gained access to the "intimacies of childbirth."[41] Accessing a woman in childbirth violates intimacy for two reasons. First, such access involves the woman's undressed body; in our society, access to the body is often used as a sign of emotional closeness. Second, access is also gained to the process of childbirth itself, access that presupposes the closest of emotional ties. Similarly, *Melvin v. Reid* did not focus on the plaintiff's embarrassment. *Melvin* involved privacy considerations because the defendant disseminated *intimate,* personal details about the plaintiff's former life as a prostitute, thus allowing others to gain *intimate informational access* to the plaintiff's life.[42] Such details about an agent's past life are intimate because they are commonly imbued with emotional significance as far as their sharing is concerned; typically, we share secrets about our past with those for whom we feel love, care, or liking. As we see in the leading cases of *De May* and *Melvin,* analysis of tort privacy law does not support Prosser's contention that the tort of privacy does not cohere around any shared concept; rather, we discover that tort privacy claims about intrusion or reputation focus on intimate physical or informational access. Rather than Prosser's disparate group of intrusion and reputation issues, we have unified Prosser's first three tort categories around the focus of intimate access.

Of course, much of the tort of privacy might cohere around issues of intimate access, yet still fail to be morally distinct. William Prosser argues that the tort of privacy not only fails to contain a conceptual core, but that it also involves three different moral interests, none of which are distinctive of privacy.[43] According to Prosser, when someone's seclusion is violated, she is wronged because her interest in freedom from mental distress has been damaged.[44] When we disclose embarrassing facts about another, we damage her interest in her good reputation.[45] For

Prosser, given the disparate interests protected by the tort of privacy, conceptual and moral clarity would best be served by talking directly about these interests, not our interest in privacy; we need only appeal to the right to freedom from mental distress or reputation rights in order to fully understand the wrong involved in reputation and intrusion tort privacy violations.

Prosser's reductionist strategy fails in its attempt to undermine the moral distinctness of reputation and intrusion tort privacy claims. It is true that tort privacy often provides a legal remedy for cases that involve mental distress or reputation damage; for example, the tort of privacy would offer me a potential legal remedy if another were to publish embarrassing facts contained in my diary, causing me both mental distress and reputation damage. However, harm done to thoughts or reputation is not the gravamen of reputation or intrusion tort privacy cases. Rather, intimacy is the morally relevant aspect of such tort privacy claims. According to tort law, it is *because* certain forms of access are intimate and, hence, valued, that the agent is provided privacy with respect to them. Hence, the moral wrong involved in violating reputation or intrusion tort privacy lies in the fact that such violations impinge upon an agent's zone of emotional intimacy, not in the fact that such violations infringe upon her reputation or mental peace (though such damage is often a by-product of damage to the zone of intimacy). To illustrate this, consider the privacy cases I have discussed previously, *De May v. Roberts* and *Melvin v. Reid*.

In *De May v. Roberts,* the court argued that it is wrong to violate the privacy of childbirth through physical intrusion. This wrong was not attributed to the fact that women bearing children presumably often feel mental distress if others intrude into their seclusion; *De May* offers no suggestion that childbearing women merit privacy only if they are likely to suffer mental distress from its lack. In fact, if the plaintiff in *De May* had felt no mental distress whatsoever, her privacy would have still been damaged. The court contended that access to childbirth merits privacy *because* of its intimacy; hence, the wrong done in *De May* involves damaging an agent's zone of intimacy, damage that may or may not cause mental distress. By gaining intimate access to the plaintiff's body, the defendant failed to respect the emotional significance our culture (including the plaintiff) places on displaying the body to others, in other words, the defendant failed to respect the plaintiff's claim to control intimate access to herself, the control protected by privacy. Because the court understood allowing access to the body, especially the body in childbirth, as a potent symbol of affection, the court placed a positive value on protecting the agent's control over such intimate access. Thus, damage to intimacy constitutes the gravamen of *De May*.

Melvin v. Reid held that it is wrong to violate another's privacy by publicizing personal facts about her past. The core of this wrong was not attributed merely to the fact that such publicity necessarily damages the reputation of the plaintiff. Given the logic of *Melvin*, it is conceivable that the plaintiff might have had exceptionally understanding acquaintances, acquaintances that would not have allowed information about her past to disturb her present reputation; such understanding friends would not have overturned the plaintiff's claim to privacy. In *Melvin,* the plaintiff's contention was that personal details about her past life should be protected by privacy *because* of their intimacy. When another attains informational access to such facts, the wrong done lies in the fact that the plaintiff's autonomy with respect to intimate informational access has not been acknowledged (a wrong that may, though not necessarily, cause harm to the plaintiff's reputation). By gaining access to intimate information about the plaintiff's past, the defendant failed to respect the emotional significance we place on sharing many details about our past with others: we commonly share details about our past with those to whom we are tied by love, care, or liking. When someone intrudes into our past, they fail to acknowledge the emotion-laden value we accord to the sharing of much information about our past. The *Melvin* court placed a positive value on protecting the agent's control over intimate information because it understood such control as central to the agent's sense of herself as a being with control over the boundaries of intimacy.

At this point, my discussion is open to a serious objection: I have unified Prosser's categories only through exclusion. I have shown that Prosser's intrusion and reputation categories are both coherent and distinct, due to their focus on the value we accord to regulating intimate access. But Prosser argued for a category I have not discussed: he argued that certain tort privacy cases involve neither intrusion nor reputation, but involve "appropriation, for the defendant's advantage, of the plaintiff's name or likeness."[46] However, this category does not seem to cohere around intimate access. Furthermore, its moral crux seems unrelated to the violation of intimacy. Consider a case that falls within its scope: the plaintiff in *Pavesich v. New England Life Insurance Company* argued that his privacy was violated when his photograph was used to sell life insurance. Yet, what links the *commercial* appropriation of a photographic image to intimate access? Apparently nothing. The question of whether appropriation is "for the defendant's advantage" clearly has no connection with intimacy or access. If the *Pavesich* court had been concerned simply with access to the plaintiff's image, they would not have focused on the commercial use of that image. Furthermore, even if the court had focused only on the dissemination of the plaintiff's image, distributing an image suitable for advertising purposes hardly seems to be a case of intimate access. Such an image is not commonly imbued with emotional significance as far as its sharing is concerned. Finally, even if we were to assume that commercially appropriating an image or name constitutes intimate access, this would only tell us that intimate access was the conceptual focus of this tort category, not the moral focus. If our name or image is appropriated, the crux of the wrong seems clear: it involves infringing upon property rights over the person and images of that person, not infringing upon intimacy.

Rather than rejecting the argument that intimate access is unrelated to Prosser's final tort category, I accept it. I agree that Prosser's category of commercial image or name appropriation is unrelated to intimate access. Attaching a price to a name or image is unrelated to its intimacy; even more tellingly, a name or image is not necessarily intimate. Even if the appropriation of a name were to constitute intimate access, Prosser's appropriation category is clearly concerned with the moral wrong attendant upon violating property rights, not intimacy claims. However, these points do not show that my argument about the coherence and distinctness of tort privacy collapses. Prosser's fourth privacy tort category simply needs to be slightly reshaped in order to accord with the conceptual and normative interests at the core of other divisions of the tort. This final category has developed out of the reasonable observation that appropriating another's name or image is *sometimes* an instance of intimate access. Furthermore, such appropriation is often wrong due to the *intimacy* of the access. This is readily illustrated. When I learn someone's pet name, I obtain intimate informational access to them. When I take a picture of someone after their beloved friend has died, I also obtain intimate access to them. In both of these cases, such details about an agent's life are intimate because they are commonly imbued with emotional significance as far as their sharing is concerned. Typically, we share secrets about our pet names with those we care for; we allow people to be around us in our grief when we feel emotional connection with them. We place a positive value on protecting our privacy with respect to such a name or image because we understand close access to these things to be morally comparable to access to a woman's person in childbirth and access to personal details about another's past: each form of access draws its meaning and value from the agent's love, liking, or care. From this intimate-access foundation, the courts have gone on to conflate intimate access with commercial access, allowing Prosser's fourth category to conceptually drift to the extent that it has indeed become a distinct tort. This drift is suggested by *Pavesich; Pavesich* appeals to not only the commercial use of an image, but also the fact that the plaintiff lost control over *access* to his *intimate* image.[47] Similarly, although the plaintiff was able to appeal only due to the commercial value of his image, the *Pavesich* court never suggest that the harm done to the agent's privacy could be remedied by providing him with financial reimbursement indexed to the commercial value of his photograph.[48] Such judicial schizophrenia suggests that Prosser's fourth privacy tort category needs the clarification an intimacy-based account of privacy can provide. Hence, I suggest that we should restore the conceptual coherence and moral distinctness of this category by restricting it to guard against only intimate appropriation of names or images.

Stepping back from Prosser's categories, does understanding privacy's value in terms of intimacy allow us to understand the foundation of tort privacy law, Warren and Brandeis's article, ''The Right to Privacy''? Given Prosser's characterization of the value of privacy, we would expect Warren and Brandeis to focus on the damage done by privacy violations to reputation, mental tranquility, and property. However, Warren and Brandeis explicitly reject this focus. They claim that mental distress might be an element of damages in privacy cases, but that privacy claims exist apart from mental distress.[49] They also disavow any necessary ties between ''material'' harms to reputation or property and privacy violations.[50] Instead, they locate the interest protected by privacy in the agent's ''inviolate personality.'' Given my account of privacy and its ties to intimacy, Warren and Brandeis's ''inviolate personality'' is based upon a principle of respect for agents as autonomous beings capable of intimacy. This interpretation is supported by the fact that Warren and Brandeis are explicitly concerned with regulating *intimate* access and information. An inviolate personality requires that we have control over access to the ''domestic circle'' and ''private life'' and control over information that ''is whispered in the closet,'' such as information about "the details of sexual relations."[51] By failing to respect another's control over such intimate information and access, we commit a "spiritual" wrong by damaging her "own feelings."[52] Privacy violations damage the agent's "own feelings" since they fail to acknowledge her autonomy with respect to love, care, and liking. Such violations constitute "spiritual" rather than "material" wrongs because they necessarily produce the intrinsic, though intangible, harm of failing to respect another as a person in the emotional sense, although they do not necessarily lead to Prosser's material harms.

By examining both specific tort privacy cases and the theoretical underpinnings of the tort of privacy contained in Warren and Brandeis's article, it is clear that we cannot explain the value accorded to the tort of privacy in terms of emotional distress, fear for reputation, and property claims. The violation of privacy might cause emotional distress, but not in all cases; it might damage someone's reputation, but not necessarily; violations might accompany damage to property claims, but this is also only a contingent link. The necessary link between privacy violations and harm consists of intimacy. In developing the tort of privacy, the courts have developed a tort that protects our interest in intimacy, our interest in being able to regulate intimate access to ourselves so as to maintain control over our expression of loving, caring, and liking. Thus, intimate access is the conceptually and morally relevant feature of the bulk of tort privacy, excluding only some of the cases that fall within the scope of Prosser's fourth tort category.

Having shown that both tort and constitutional privacy possess a conceptual and normative focus based on intimacy, one final question remains: is tort privacy compatible with constitutional privacy? Tort and constitutional privacy have been accused of embodying radically different accounts of the function, content, and value of privacy. Tort privacy has been interpreted as resting on separation, matters of access, and the value of being left alone. According to this interpretation, tort privacy is the state of our having personal information or experience separated from the senses of others; we value this state because we value being left alone. Constitutional privacy has been linked to control, intimate decisions, and the value of possessing autonomy. According to this interpretation, privacy is the state of our having control over decisions about our intimate actions; we value this state because we value autonomy.

The apparent tension between tort and constitutional privacy's function, content, and value is easily resolved. As far as the function of privacy is concerned, both tort and constitutional privacy work through control. This is readily apparent in the case of constitutional privacy; the constitutional right to privacy "turns on some form of substantive liberty or autonomy."[53] However, privacy has commonly been interpreted as a state of separation in tort privacy law since tort cases involve separating the agent from public access (e.g., *De May* involved the plaintiff's claim that she should have been separated from the defendant who accessed her in childbirth, and *Melvin* involved the plaintiff's claim that information about her past as a prostitute should have been kept separate from the public sphere). But, as I have discussed, separation need not be antithetical to control. Cases such as *De May* and *Melvin* do not involve the state protecting the agent's privacy by ensuring that she is accessed by none; they involve the state allowing the agent to control her sphere of intimacy by separating herself from intimate access by others. Hence, tort privacy also provides the agent with control, which manifests itself in a state of separation between the plaintiff and other parties. As for the content of privacy, tort privacy protects decisions about intimate access, whereas constitutional privacy protects decisions about intimate activities; however, this difference does not reveal a conceptual conflict between these areas of law. Since privacy protects an agent's control over intimate decisions as a whole, tort and constitutional privacy simply protect different subsets of this central set of intimate decisions.[54] Finally, as far as the value of privacy is concerned, I have argued that tort and constitutional privacy both acknowledge the value we accord to protecting the agent's autonomy with respect to emotional intimacy. In short, although the concerns of Estelle Griswold, Samuel Warren, and Louis Brandeis may appear unrelated, they shared a common desire to protect the agent's "inviolate personality" with respect to intimacy.

Notes

1. Samuel Warren and Louis Brandeis, "The Right to Privacy," *The Harvard Law Review* 4 (1890): 196.

2. Griswold v. Connecticut, 381 U.S. 479 (1965).

3. For a systematic discussion of the legal cases associated with tort privacy law, see William Prosser's article, "Privacy," *California Law Review* 48 (1960): 383–422.

4. See Bowers v. Hardwick, 85 U.S. 140 (1986), for a list of the cases associated with these matters.

5. Hyman Gross, "The Concept of Privacy," *New York University Law Review* 42 (1967): 34–54.

6. At this point, I might be charged with circularity: given that I have used intuitions from privacy law in constructing my definition of privacy, how can I turn around and use my privacy definition to critique privacy law? However, this criticism does not hold. Clearly we can generate a general claim, such as a claim about the mathematical relation that holds between a group of numbers, and use it to make descriptive claims about previously unmentioned terms of the sequence and prescriptive claims about what terms ought to appear in the sequence as it progresses. Similarly, I am using my general claim about the nature of privacy to make descriptive and prescriptive claims about privacy law.

7. Ferdinand Schoeman introduces the use of "coherence" and "distinctness" in "Privacy: Philosophical Dimensions," *American Philosophical Quarterly* 21 (1984): 200. Rather than allowing more terminology to proliferate, I will use Schoeman's clear terms in this chapter.

8. See, for example, Gross, "The Concept of Privacy," 34.

9. See, for example, Louis Henkin, "Privacy and Autonomy," *Columbia Law Review* 74 (1974): 1410.

10. See Bowers v. Hardwick, majority opinion.

11. See, respectively, Griswold v. Connecticut; Loving v. Virginia, 388 U.S. 1 (1967); Stanley v. Georgia, 394 U.S. 557 (1969).

12. Griswold v. Connecticut, majority opinion.

13. See David A. J. Richards, "The Jurisprudence of Privacy as a Constitutional Right," in *Privacy,* ed. William Bier (New York: Fordham University Press, 1980), 149.

14. Roe v. Wade, 410 U.S. 113 (1973), majority opinion.

15. Paris Adult Theatre I v. Slaton, U.S. 413 (1973), majority opinion.

16. Note that the liberty I will be referring to throughout this chapter is more fully described as "the liberty to pursue your life without undue state regulation"—for the sake of convenience, I will often refer to it as simply "liberty."

17. Gross, "The Concept of Privacy," 50.

18. Richards, "The Jurisprudence of Privacy as a Constitutional Right," 140.

19. For example, see Henkin, "Privacy and Autonomy," 1410.

20. Roe v. Wade, majority opinion.

21. Roe v. Wade, dissenting opinion.

22. Judith DeCew, "Defending the 'Private' in Constitutional Privacy," *The Journal of Value Inquiry* 21 (1987): 183.

23. Griswold v. Connecticut, majority opinion.

24. Paris Adult Theatre I v. Slaton, majority opinion.

25. See Richards, "The Jurisprudence of Privacy as a Constitutional Right," 149.

26. Roe v. Wade, majority opinion.

27. Roe v. Wade, majority opinion; quote taken from Brennan's opinion in Eisenstadt v. Baird, 405 U.S. 438 (1972).

28. In this argument about *Roe,* all I have shown is that women have a privacy interest with respect to abortion due to the link between having a child and intimacy. This, of course, ignores the possibility that the fetus might have interests of its own. If this were the case, clearly the mother's interest in privacy would have to be weighed in comparison to the fetus' interests. Since I have shown that the mother has a prima facie claim to an abortion, the burden of proof is now placed upon opponents of abortion to establish the interests of the fetus.

29. Stanley v. Georgia, majority opinion.

30. Paris Adult Theatre I v. Slaton, majority opinion.

31. See Bowers v. Hardwick, majority opinion.

32. In the words of the Court: "This case does not require a judgment on whether laws against sodomy between consenting adults in general . . . are wise and desirable" (see Bowers v. Hardwick, majority opinion).

33. Bowers v. Hardwick, majority opinion.

34. Bowers v. Hardwick, Blackmun's dissenting opinion.

35. This might be a charitable reading of the Court's confusion. It is based upon the tacit assumption that the Court has simply failed to recognize that intimacy links together previous privacy issues with issues of homosexual sexuality. This presupposes that the Court would accept the link between homosexual sexuality and the love, liking, and care constitutive of intimacy. However, the Court seems to reject this link since it compares homosexual activity to "incest, and other sexual crimes" (see Bowers v. Hardwick, majority opinion). Clearly this position stems from nothing more defensible than bias.

36. For an example of such criticisms, see William Prosser, "Privacy," *California Law Review* 48 (1960): 383–422.

37. The discussion which follows is indebted to Edward Bloustein's important article "Privacy as an Aspect of Human Dignity." See Edward Bloustein, "Privacy as an Aspect of Human Dignity: An Answer to Dean Prosser," *New York University Law Review* 39 (1964): 962–1007. In fact, my analysis can be understood as a sympathetic attempt to expand upon the promise of Bloustein's analysis. Bloustein links the value of privacy to the vague notion of "human dignity." Although I find this a promising start, it immediately raises questions: How should we define "human dignity"? Does privacy protect all aspects of human dignity? I believe that privacy protects human dignity only when intimacy is at stake. Hence, my account of privacy possesses a narrower scope than Bloustein's account.

38. Prosser, "Privacy," 389.

39. I have decided to discuss these well-known cases so that readers can compare my analysis of these cases with other discussions of the same cases, especially Edward Bloustein's "Privacy as an Aspect of Human Dignity." De May v. Roberts, 46 Mich. 160, 9 N.W. 146 (1981); Melvin v. Reid, 112 Cal. App. 285, 297 P. 91 (1931); Pavesich v. New England Life Insurance Company, 122 Ga. 190, 50 S.E. 68 (1905). Since I fully accept Prosser's argument that public disclosure and "false light" cases share a common foundation, interest in reputation, I do not discuss these categories separately in what follows (see Prosser, "Privacy," note 18). Hence, I do not discuss any tort privacy cases involving "false light issues."

40. De May v. Roberts, majority opinion.

41. Edward Bloustein, "Privacy as an Aspect of Human Dignity."

42. Melvin v. Reid, majority opinion.

43. Prosser, "Privacy," 389. I only discuss three moral interests, since Prosser's four distinct privacy torts rest on only three distinct moral interests; see note 25.

44. Prosser, "Privacy," 392.

45. Prosser, "Privacy," 401.

46. Prosser, "Privacy," 389.

47. Pavesich v. New England Life Insurance Company, majority opinion.

48. In fact, if the plaintiff's identical image had appeared in a newspaper story rather than in a commercial advertisement, he would have had no legal claim against the publisher. I am indebted to an anonymous reviewer of this book for making this important point.

49. Warren and Brandeis, "The Right to Privacy," 198.

50. Warren and Brandeis, "The Right to Privacy," 197, 214.

51. Warren and Brandeis, "The Right to Privacy," 196.

52. Warren and Brandeis, "The Right to Privacy," 197.

53. Richards, "The Jurisprudence of Privacy as a Constitutional Right," 140.

54. Hence, a reductionist strategy designed to eliminate either tort or constitutional privacy law will necessarily eliminate something of value. In other words, while tort and constitutional privacy law are conceptually compatible, they are not identical in the protection they extend.

9

In Conclusion: Answers and New Questions

Throughout this book, I have referred to the elusive status of privacy and the chaotic state of the legal and philosophical privacy literature. Having now reached the final chapter, I am faced with three questions: Have the legal and philosophical questions concerning privacy raised in the second chapter been answered? Does my account of privacy give rise to any questions of its own? If so, do these new questions establish that my account of privacy leaves us with nothing more than the chaotic, elusive concept with which this work began? In what follows, I answer these questions. After sketching how my control and intimacy-based account of privacy responds to the questions contained in Chapter 2, I acknowledge that my account of privacy gives rise to a host of new questions; but these questions do not contribute to the chaos of privacy theory—they merely indicate that the project of placing privacy into a broader philosophical context remains to be undertaken. I conclude by noting some of the avenues of research that have been opened by my definition of privacy and explanation of its value.

The debates about privacy found in the legal and philosophical literature were organized into three categories in Chapter 2: questions about the definition of privacy; questions concerning the value of privacy; questions about the conceptual and moral distinctness of privacy. The questions in each of these categories have been answered by my account of privacy.

The problem of how to define privacy was broken into two questions. Does privacy function through control or separation? Does privacy's content cover information about an agent, access to an agent, or the agent's freedom of intimate action? As I have shown, privacy functions through control; a privacy claim is a claim to have control over a realm of life. This is not to deny that separation may play a role in privacy. Control often manifests itself through separation; for example, if I separate myself from others, it is probable that I will acquire a greater degree of control over the information others learn about me than I possessed while in their company. Instances of separation only possess the potential to be instances of privacy to the extent that they are manifestations of control. Turning to the content of privacy, privacy's scope cannot be limited to either information, access, or the intimate decisions protected by constitutional privacy law—it includes all three. What unites these apparently disparate areas is the common denominator of intimacy. Privacy protects the agent's control over decisions about intimate information concerning herself, decisions about intimate access to herself, and decisions about her own intimate actions.

Two questions also developed concerning privacy's value. What value is accorded to privacy? Does privacy's value stem from its consequences or from a principle of respect for persons? Privacy is accorded a necessarily positive value. Although it undeniably promotes desirable consequences—enabling intimacy between individuals to flourish— these consequences are not the root of privacy's value. Yet neither does that value stem from a principle of respect for persons as rational choosers. We value privacy because we value respecting others as persons in the emotional sense, persons with the capacity for love, care, and liking. Privacy embodies this respect by protecting the autonomy of agents with respect to their expression of love, liking, and care.

There were two skeptical questions raised about privacy. Is privacy conceptually distinct? Is privacy morally distinct? Judith Jarvis Thomson answered both of these questions in the negative, yet an affirmative answer is more true to the nature of privacy. Privacy claims are conceptually distinct from liberty claims or property claims (the type of claims under which they are most often subsumed) because they cohere around intimacy. Hence, claims concerning liberty with respect to intimacy may be privacy claims, but privacy claims cannot justifiably be collapsed into liberty claims. Similarly, claims concerning intimate property may be privacy claims, but all property claims are not privacy claims. As far as the moral distinctness of privacy is concerned, intimacy also comes into play; we value privacy not merely because it provides us with liberty or control over our property, but because it provides us with control over intimacy.

Let me finally draw together the pieces of my account of privacy, presenting both my final definition of privacy and my explanation of its positive value. My definition of privacy consists of two parts—the function and content of privacy. Privacy functions through control, while its content ranges over decisions concerning intimate access to the agent, intimate information about the agent, and intimate actions on the agent's part (that is, constitutional privacy matters). Placing these together, we arrive at my preliminary definition of privacy: privacy is the state of possessing control over a realm of intimate decisions, which includes decisions about intimate access, intimate information, and intimate actions.

But what constitutes intimacy? Intimacy is not a product of behavior. It is a product of the agent's love, liking, and care for others. To claim that an act, action, or activity is intimate is to claim that it draws its meaning and value for the agent from her love, liking, or care. Decisions are intimate when they concern such intimate matters. This account of intimacy allows us to produce a final definition of privacy: privacy is the state of possessing control over decisions concerning matters that draw their meaning and value from the agent's love, liking, and care. In other words, claims to privacy are claims to possess autonomy with respect to love, liking, and care. As far as the positive value of privacy is concerned, it stems from a particular understanding of what respect for persons as moral beings demands. If we understand personhood in terms of the agent's capacity for love, liking, and care (as well as rationality), respect for personhood entails acknowledging the agent's autonomy with reference to these capacities. Assuming that we value respecting others as moral persons, we must place a positive value on privacy, as it protects this sphere of autonomy surrounding intimacy.

My account of privacy succeeds in at least one fashion: it responds to the questions I originally raised concerning privacy's existence, definition, and value. However, my responses do not lay all questions to rest. Questions arise with respect to every aspect of privacy. In particular, questions can be raised about my definition of privacy, my account of privacy's value, my refutation of skepticism concerning privacy, and the application of my privacy theory to everyday privacy issues. First, consider my privacy definition. I argued that privacy is the state of possessing control over intimate decisions, but I only briefly discussed control. Hence, much remains to be spelled out with respect to the question of what conditions must hold if we are to justifiably claim that an agent possesses control over a given action. Second, I suggested that the value of privacy stems from a principle of respect for persons as beings with the capacity to love, like, and care. But this gives rise to questions about both the liberal account of human nature and the nature of emotions. Why should we acknowledge an agent's capacity for love, liking, and care as an essential human capacity? Are other emotional states equally essential to personhood? How should we distinguish between love, liking, and care? What constitutes an expression of these emotions? Third, I argued that there is no justification for skepticism with regard to the existence of privacy *claims*. But what about skepticism with regard to a *right* to privacy? And fourth, I revealed that my account of privacy provides a theoretical foundation for the privacy claims found in the legal realm without extensively discussing the ramifications of my theory as far as the future development of privacy law is concerned. Hence various questions about the theory and application of privacy law remain to be answered, for example, should we have secrecy laws as well as privacy laws? If constitutional privacy protects reproductive intimacy, should activities such as surrogate mothering fall within its domain? Is a right to privacy compatible with standards of constitutional interpretation? As these questions indicate, my account of privacy may have answered certain questions, but it has raised a surfeit of new ones in the process. Can my privacy account escape the criticism that it only *contributes* to the chaos surrounding privacy?

The above questions do not constitute an attempt to *undermine* my privacy theory. Instead they seek to place my account of privacy within a broader philosophical context than that provided in the course of this work. The questions about what constitutes control reveal a need to situate privacy in a theory of human action. The question about whether there is such a thing as a right to privacy shows that privacy could be illuminated further by a theory of rights. The questions concerning the respect we accord to persons as loving, caring, and liking beings show that privacy demands both a liberal theory of human nature and a theory of emotion. Finally, the questions about the application of privacy theory to the legal sphere show that privacy theory must be positioned alongside of an account of legal practice. These examples reveal that my account of privacy leads us onto paths that extend far beyond privacy: theories of human action, human nature, emotion, rights, and the law. It does not abandon us in the chaos in which we began.

This book began at one starting point, only to conclude at yet another starting point. In the process, it presented a control and intimacy-based definition of privacy. It also linked the value of privacy to a principle of respect for persons as beings with the capacity to love, care, and like—beings with the capacity for close interpersonal relationships. However, progress in this book has taken the form of creating new questions from old ones, rather than settling all privacy debates. Thus, it is appropriate for me to conclude with a question rather than an answer: what account of human action, human nature, emotion, rights, and legal practice does privacy presuppose, require, or dictate?

SELECTED BIBLIOGRAPHY

Allen, Anita. *Uneasy Access: Privacy for Women in a Free Society.* New Jersey: Rowman and Littlefield, 1988.

———. "Women and Their Privacy: What Is at Stake?" In *Beyond Domination: New Perspectives on Women and Philosophy,* ed. Carol Gould, 233–49. New York: Rowman and Allanheld, 1984.

Andre, Judith. "Privacy as a Value and as a Right." *The Journal of Value Inquiry* 20 (1986): 309–17.

Beardsley, Elizabeth. "Privacy: Autonomy and Selective Disclosure." In *Privacy: Nomos XIII,* ed. J. Roland Pennock and John W. Chapman, 56–70. New York: Atherton Press, 1971.

Benn, Stanley. "Privacy, Freedom, and Respect for Persons." In *Privacy: Nomos XIII,* ed. J. Roland Pennock and John W. Chapman, 1–26. New York: Atherton Press, 1971.

———. "Privacy and Respect for Persons: A Reply." *The Australian Journal of Philosophy* 58 (1980): 54–61.

———. "Protection and Limitation of Privacy." *Australian Law Journal* 52 (1978): 601–12.

Benn, Stanley, and Gerald Gaus, ed. *The Public and the Private in Social Policy.* London: Croom Helm and St. Martin's Press, 1983.

Bier, William, ed. *Privacy.* New York: Fordham University Press, 1980.

Bloustein, Edward. *Individual and Group Privacy.* New Jersey: Transaction Books, 1978.

———. "Privacy as an Aspect of Human Dignity: An Answer to Dean Prosser." *New York University Law Review* 39 (1964): 962–1007.

Bok, Sissela. *Secrets: On the Ethics of Concealment and Revelation.* New York: Random House, 1983.

Bronaugh, Richard, ed. *Philosophical Law: Authority, Equality, Adjudication and Privacy.* Westport, CT: Greenwood Press, 1978.

Chapman, John. "Personality and Privacy." In *Privacy: Nomos XIII,* ed. J. Roland Pennock and John W. Chapman, 236–55. New York: Atherton Press, 1971.

Chapman, John, and J. Roland Pennock, eds. *Privacy: Nomos XIII.* New York: Atherton Press, 1971.

Clark, Lorenne. "Privacy, Property, Freedom, and the Family." In *Philosophi-*

cal Law, ed. Richard Bronaugh, 167–87. Westport, CT: Greenwood Press, 1978.

Davis, Frederick. "What Do We Mean by 'Right to Privacy'?" *South Dakota Law Review* 4 (1959): 1–24.

DeCew, Judith. "Defending the 'Private' in Constitutional Privacy." *The Journal of Value Inquiry* 21 (1987): 171–84.

———. "The Scope of Privacy in Law and Ethics." *Law and Philosophy* 5 (1986): 145–73.

Dionisopoulos, P. Allan, and Craig Ducat. *The Right to Privacy: Essays and Cases.* St. Paul: West Publishing Co., 1976.

Dixon, Robert, Jr. "The Griswold Penumbra: Constitutional Charter for an Expanded Law of Privacy?" *Michigan Law Review* 64 (1965): 197–231.

Doss, Arden, and Diane Kay Doss. "On Morals, Privacy, and the Constitution." *University of Miami Law Review* 25 (1971): 395–419.

Dworkin, Gerald. "Privacy and the Law." In *Privacy,* ed. John Young, 113–36. New York: John Wiley and Sons, 1978.

Eichbaum, June. "Towards an Autonomy-Based Theory of Constitutional Privacy: Beyond the Ideology of Familial Privacy." *Harvard Civil Rights–Civil Liberties Law Review* 14 (1979): 361–84.

Ely, Jack. "The Wages of Crying Wolf: A Comment on Roe v. Wade." *Yale Law Journal* 82 (1973): 920–84.

Freund, Paul. "Privacy: One Concept or Many?" In *Privacy: Nomos XIII,* ed. J. Roland Pennock and John W. Chapman, 182–98. New York: Atherton Press, 1971.

Fried, Charles. *An Anatomy of Values.* London: Oxford University Press, 1970.

———. "Privacy." *Yale Law Journal* 77 (1968): 475–93.

Garrett, Roland. "The Nature of Privacy." *Philosophy Today* 18 (1974): 263–84.

Gavison, Ruth. "Privacy and the Limits of Law." *Yale Law Journal* 89 (1980): 421–72.

Gerety, Tom. "Redefining Privacy." *Harvard Civil Rights–Civil Liberties Law Review* 12 (1977): 233–96.

Gerstein, Robert. "Intimacy and Privacy." *Ethics* 89 (1978): 86–91.

———. "Privacy and Self-Incrimination." *Ethics* 80 (1970): 87–101.

Grcic, Joseph. "The Right to Privacy: Behavior as Property." *Journal of Value Inquiry* 20 (1986): 137–44.

Gross, Hyman. "The Concept of Privacy." *New York University Law Review* 42 (1967): 34–54.

———. "Privacy and Autonomy." In *Privacy: Nomos XIII,* ed. J. Roland Pennock and John W. Chapman, 169–81. New York: Atherton Press, 1971.

Henkin, Louis. "Privacy and Autonomy." *Columbia Law Review* 74 (1974): 1410–33.

Hixson, Richard. *Privacy in a Public Society.* New York: Oxford University Press, 1987.

Jaggar, Alison. "Love and Knowledge: Emotion in Feminist Epistemology." In *Women, Knowledge, and Reality,* ed. Ann Garry and Marilyn Pearsall, 129–55. Boston: Unwin Hyman, 1989.

Kalven, Harry, Jr. "Privacy in Tort Law: Were Warren and Brandeis Wrong?" 31 *Law and Contemporary Problems* 31 (1966): 326–41.

Karafiel, Emile. "The Right of Privacy and the Sidis Case." *Georgia Law Review* 12 (1978): 513–34.

Karst, Kenneth. "The Freedom of Intimate Association." *Yale Law Journal* 89 (1980): 624–92.

Keith, Boone. "Privacy and Community." *Social Theory and Practice* 9 (1983): 1–33.

Konvitz, Milton. "Privacy and the Law: A Philosophical Prelude." *Law and Contemporary Problems* 31 (1966): 272–80.

Kupfer, Joseph. "Privacy, Autonomy, and Self-Concept." *American Philosophical Quarterly* 24 (1987): 81–88.

Levine, Morton. "Privacy in the Tradition of the Western World." In *Privacy,* ed. William Bier, 3–21. New York: Fordham University Press, 1980.

Lusky, Louis. "Invasion of Privacy: A Clarification of Concepts." *Columbia Law Review* 72 (1972): 693–710.

MacKinnon, Catharine. "Privacy v. Equality: Beyond Roe v. Wade." In MacKinnon, *Feminism UnModified.* Boston: Harvard University Press, 1987.

McCloskey, H. J. "Privacy and the Right to Privacy." *Philosophy* 55 (1980): 17–38.

———. "The Political Ideal of Privacy." *The Philosophical Quarterly* 21 (1971): 303–14.

Mill, John Stuart. *On Liberty.* Indianapolis: Hackett Publishing, 1978.

Moore, Barrington. *Privacy: Studies in Social and Cultural History.* New York: M. E. Sharpe, 1984.

Neville, Robert. "Various Meanings of Privacy: A Philosophical Analysis." In *Privacy,* ed. William Bier, 22–34. New York: Fordham University Press, 1980.

O'Brien, David. *Privacy, Law, and Public Policy.* New York: Praeger, 1979.

O'Neill, Onora. "Between Consenting Adults." *Philosophy and Public Affairs* 14 (1985): 252–77.

Parent, William A. "A New Definition of Privacy for the Law." *Law and Philosophy* 2 (1983): 305–38.

———. "Privacy, Morality, and the Law." *Philosophy and Public Affairs* 12 (1983): 269–88.

———. "Recent Work on the Concept of Privacy." *American Philosophical Quarterly* 20 (1983): 341–55.

Parker, Richard. "A Definition of Privacy." *Rutgers Law Review* 27 (1974): 275–96.

Posner, Richard. "The Right to Privacy." *Georgia Law Review* 12 (1974): 393–422.

———. "Uncertain Protection of Privacy By the Supreme Court." *Supreme Court Review* (1979): 173–216.

Prosser, William. "Privacy." *California Law Review* 48 (1960): 383–422.

Rachels, James. "Why Privacy Is Important." *Philosophy and Public Affairs* 4 (1975): 323–33.

Rehnquist, William H. "Is an Expanded Right to Privacy Consistent with Fair and Effective Law Enforcement?" 23 *Kansas Law Review* 1 (1974): 1–22.

Reiman, Jeffrey. "Privacy, Intimacy and Personhood." *Philosophy and Public Affairs* 6 (1976): 26–44.

Richards, David A. J. "Constitutional Privacy, Religious Disestablishment, and the Abortion Decisions." In *Abortion,* ed. Jay Garfield and Patricia Hennessey, 148–74. Amherst, MA: University of Massachusetts Press, 1984.

———. "The Jurisprudence of Privacy as a Constitutional Right." In *Privacy,* ed. William Bier, 135–51. New York: Fordham University Press, 1980.

———. *Toleration and the Constitution.* New York: Oxford University Press, 1986.

———. "Unnatural Acts and the Constitutional Right to Privacy: A Moral Theory." *Fordham Law Review* 45 (1977): 1312–48.

Rubenfeld, Jed. "The Right of Privacy." *Harvard Law Review* 102 (1989): 737–807.

Scanlon, Thomas. "Thomson on Privacy." *Philosophy and Public Affairs* 4 (1975): 315–22.

Schneider, Carl. *Shame, Exposure and Privacy.* Boston: Beacon Press, 1977.

Schoeman, Ferdinand, ed. *Philosophical Dimensions of Privacy: An Anthology.* New York: Cambridge University Press, 1984.

———. "Privacy and Intimate Information." In *Philosophical Dimensions of Privacy: An Anthology,* ed. Ferdinand Schoeman, 403–18. New York: Cambridge University Press, 1984.

———. "Privacy: Philosophical Dimensions." *American Philosophical Quarterly* 21 (1984): 199–213.

Shils, Edward. *The Torment of Secrecy.* New York: Free Press, 1956.

Spelman, Elizabeth. "Anger and Insubordination." In *Women, Knowledge, and Reality,* ed. Ann Garry and Marilyn Pearsall, 263–73. Boston: Unwin Hyman, 1989.

Thomson, Judith Jarvis. "The Right to Privacy." *Philosophy and Public Affairs* 4 (1975): 295–314.

Van Den Haag, Ernest. "On Privacy." In *Privacy: Nomos XIII,* ed. J. Roland Pennock and John Chapman, 149–68. New York: Atherton Press, 1971.

Wacks, Raymond. *Personal Information: Privacy and the Law.* Oxford: Clarendon Press, 1989.

———. *The Protection of Privacy.* London: Sweet & Maxwell, 1980.

Warren, Samuel, and Louis Brandeis. "The Right to Privacy." *The Harvard Law Review* 4 (1890): 193–220.

Wasserstrom, Richard. "Privacy: Some Arguments and Assumptions." In *Philosophical Law,* ed. Bronaugh, 148–66. Westport, CT: Greenwood Press, 1978.

Weinstein, W. L. "The Private and the Free: A Conceptual Inquiry." In *Privacy: Nomos XIII,* ed. J. Roland Pennock and John Chapman, 27–55. New York: Atherton Press, 1971.

Westin, Alan. *Privacy and Freedom.* New York: Atheneum, 1967.

Young, John, ed. *Privacy.* New York: John Wiley and Sons, 1978.

INDEX